Vision Power

Vision Power

The Mind's Eye:
Transforming Your Thoughts into Reality

Edward L. Keyton

Although the author has made every effort to ensure that the information in this book was correct at the time of first publication, the author does not assume and hereby disclaims any liability to any party for any loss, damage, or disruption caused by errors or omissions, whether such errors or omissions result from negligence, accident, or any other cause.

*This literary effort is a tribute to my wife, sons, and daughter,
in hopes that my efforts will inspire them to greater achievement.*

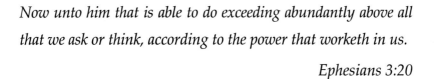

Now unto him that is able to do exceeding abundantly above all that we ask or think, according to the power that worketh in us.

Ephesians 3:20

Contents

Acknowledgments

My sincere thanks to:

Katrina Newby, who was very instrumental in the early stages of this endeavor.

Cynithia Reeder, who has helped me in many ways, including this project. Her assistance and friendship has inspired me.

Cecelia Morris, who took the time to proofread this material even when she had a load of personal challenges to face.

And, of course, my wife, whose help goes beyond the pale in helping with this project and life in general. Words cannot express the appreciation for your input, particularly your computer skills, which proved to be an invaluable asset for me.

I thank all of the people who kept asking me over and over where the book is. Thank you all; and in particular, I thank God.

Introduction

It seems as if it was only yesterday, and I can clearly remember. In 1970, I arrived in Atlanta on a Greyhound bus with seventy dollars in my pocket, a one-way ticket, and a dream of a better life. Perhaps you have heard stories like mine before; there may be many similarities between this saga and others. Some stories may even depict a harder way of life than the one I'm telling you about; however, I'm sure you have never heard my story. My desire is to share with you how I beat the odds, and the system and strategy I used to arrive at my purpose in life. This system is simple, yet powerful, and can be beneficial to anyone who takes time to read these pages. My life's account will prove especially helpful to the young and misguided who believe they know the way, but are lost and wandering—clueless and hopeless to the facts. Life is all about systems, and, if you don't have the right one working for you, the journey through this existence can be very much hit and miss.

Life experiences have taught me that every success requires a personal investment of time, energy, and research on behalf of the achiever. In order to reach one's intended purpose and destination, a certain degree of planning must also be included. Whether it is a coach's game plan for winning against the opposing team or a surgeon entering into the most common surgical procedure, every successful endeavor must have a strategy. When the goal is to succeed, even the most skilled individual understands that pursuing one's purpose without strategy can be a flawed process.

A vision works the same way. One's vision has certain mystical powers when held in view. It is first seen in the mind of the achiever, and at a certain point, with enough desire and tenacity, it will manifest externally. The achiever must have clearly defined objectives and goals, which are paramount to the realization of one's dream. When a vision is outlined and defined, it is faith in action. Faith is believing in the beauty and possibility of your vision becoming a reality. Biblically, to see one's dream inside the mind is to identify "the substance of things hoped for" (Hebrews 11:1–3). The manifestation of this dream is the evidence of things first seen inside of the mind of the dreamer. A well-known musician, Stevie Wonder, referred to this as "inner vision." A defined vision can be a fail-safe strategy to taking one from the mundane and mediocre life to a majestic and marvelous life full of joy and accomplishment; of this I am certain.

A vision is like having an internal compass that points to your desired destiny. I believe what we think about, we bring about. Keep in mind that your vision is your own personally designed dream, and you can be as innovative and imaginative as you please. You are at liberty to "call those things which be not, as though they were" (Romans 4:17). This is your vision. This idea is more than a simple concept; for you, it is a reality that, within your being and according to your faith, can be a reality when there is a plan attached to your vision—possibilities become probabilities for the manifestation of your heartfelt desires. "If thou can believe all things are possible to him that believe" (Mark 9:23). The process of visioning is doable, and it can be pleasantly surprising to those who dare to take the chance to be more calculating about the things they want in life. A vision is a blueprint that you personally design for your life—a new, more progressive, and more successful you.

Visioning is a process with roots that are as old as the creation of the universe. In the beginning, God had a plan and the power to bring about human creation. He saw it, designed it, spoke it, and it became (Genesis 1). I'm yearning to show you this process with hopes that you might access this great power just as I have. The process of visioning is not a secret; however, it is hidden from the nonreader and those who no longer dream and hope for a better life. It is hidden from the impatient individual who would rather rob, steal, and kill, as opposed to think, plan, and act on their dreams. When this process is used as instructed, it is mind-blowing and life-changing. If you want to change your life for the better in every aspect, I pray you would allow me the privilege to assist you in developing a more creative, dynamic you.

In the Holy Bible, the book of Habakkuk 2:2, the Lord told the prophet, "Write the vision and make it plain." Writing your dream and vision gives it life, hope, and purpose. *Vision Power* is all about taking you to the next level in designing your life; be specific about what you want. Come, let us go on this journey together as you prepare for new discoveries in designing your vision. But you have to leave doubt, fear, and mediocrity behind and give God the glory!

While on this journey, you will be able to understand the process of constructing your dream through vision, strategy, and purpose. You will also be offered the opportunity to identify any habits that you might have that are preventing you from reaching your full potential. It is necessary to read each chapter in sequential order, so your mindset will begin to transform as you move through each section. Make sure you keep a journal to record your incredible journey as you become the person you were meant to be; your life will be positively changed forever. It is my desire that after you have read *Vision Power* and completed your journey, you will have been encouraged and enlightened. I also hope that you will find yourself having risen to new heights and new expectations that will point you to your destiny.

Whether you are a young man or a young woman, understand this: if you have patience and purpose, life can be good to you. However, without patience and purpose, you are headed to a bad place. I speak this from my own personal experience and also by way of observing many others as they make their way through the maze of life. Jailhouses are filled with the young and the old who had no patience; they had to have material things and the luxuries of life, fast and without personal efforts. They had no purpose or aims that were legitimately attainable, so they decided to do something quick and slick and found themselves behind bars or worse. If you have no patience and purpose and little regard for the law, there is most certainly a cell with your name on it waiting for you. What's even more interesting is that the jails and prisons are filled with people who think that they are slick and smooth. In my estimation, individuals who are truly slick do not end up in jail. Even those with the most limited education know that the jailhouse is no place to be. Achievement is not something that is exclusive to a few. You do not have to be locked out of the realm of success, and you do not have to be locked up in a cell like a wild animal.

Make your mark and make up your mind that losing your freedom or failing in life is not an option. You can start developing a legacy of nobility and leave your name behind as one of the lions of society that made your generation a better one by taking advantage of the countless opportunities that surround us all. In order to get to the top of the heap, you might need to stop running with the crowd and become the unique individual that God intended you to be—you can do it! True achievement comes in baby steps. The more you achieve, the more you believe in yourself.

The experience that *Vision Power* is offering you is more about standing out than fitting in. One reason is that it takes more guts to stand out. Visioning is all about you becoming more aware of what you can accomplish with the right thinking and the right amount of patience, purpose, and planning. You might not know what you want or what your purpose is, but I do know you can get there from here. Powerful, dynamic lives are planned; they do not just appear out of thin air.

Visioning is an exercise about finding the most powerful and productive you. It is every person's heavenly destiny to become all that God has designed them to be. When you are living up to God's given potential, you will feel more at ease and have greater clarity. Most people, it appears, do not have a clue about this truth. Many are too busy chasing another man's dream. Why not chase your own? In this American society, the emphasis is on wealth and the trappings of wealth. As individuals, we have lost sight of a higher calling in life than the gain of money. Sure, we all need it; perhaps we fail to realize that wealth is tied directly to some service rendered. There has been a great paradigm shift pertaining to money that says *just get it*. If money is the end-all for peace of mind, why do so many million-dollar lottery winners end up broke again after a few years, and why are some of them on the verge of insanity and suicide? The principle thing before the attainment of wealth is the attainment of wisdom. When we work and plan for advancement, the gain is not so easily squandered.

When you identify your dreams, desires, and the contribution you want to make, it is then that you will begin to strategize as to how to deliver the goods. You'll establish how to get what you want with integrity and without taking from another in order to satisfy yourself. The wise man Solomon had this to say about ill-gotten gain: "and they lay wait for their blood; they lurk privily for their own lives, so are the ways of every one that is greedy of gain; which taketh away the life of the owners thereof" (Proverbs 1:18–19). It is a common practice in our society for men and women to shed the blood of another for money. Balance is the element missing from our lives. There is a dark and ancient saying in the Bible in the book of Proverbs, chapter thirty, verses seven and eight. The writer asked God for help in balancing his life. He stated, "Give me enough food to live on, neither too much nor too little. If I'm too full, I might become arrogant, saying, 'God? Who needs him?' If I'm poor, I might steal and dishonor the name of my God." I believe in the word of God and His divine directives. It is a proven path to peace of mind and harmony of the soul. In this modern culture, respect for God is fading. If you are in touch with Him, the more peace you are likely to find—it is about balance.

Why go through life and not leave your mark? It is incumbent upon all to make a contribution to this society and leave it better by our efforts than how we found it. Find your purpose, what you love to do or would like to do, refine it, and make it pay you. For example, my passion is motivating people and helping them find new meaning to an otherwise boring existence, to bring smiles to faces and facilitate the attainment of peace of mind and true joy by communicating the truth of the higher power. This I love not for the money, necessarily, but because it makes me feel good to know that I have helped another weary soul to the next level of accomplishment in the divine.

Here's to a lifetime of vision!

CHAPTER 1

My Story

I know all too well about adversity, drama, and the trauma of life. As far as I know, my parents were two ships passing in the night. I was, as they say, a love child—or simply the result of unchecked passion between two young lovers who placed no thought in the possibility of their actions, producing a child from their few moments of pleasure. At fourteen years old, I met my father for the first time, and I saw him only three times after that. It seems that the sightings of my father were about every ten years.

I was raised in a rat- and roach-infested home, and with no heat or insulation in the walls or ceilings, it was brutally cold during the winter. We had one little kerosene heater in the kitchen area of the house that offered very little comfort. Our home on Aiken Street, on the outskirts of St. Augustine, Florida, was steaming hot during the summer and sometimes freezing cold in the winter. Our little three-room house was cramped in space compared to others; however, I suppose my mother did the best she could do with what she had to work with. Mother was a licensed practical nurse and one of the first African-American women in the St. Augustine area to have such a position during the 1950s. My mother later lost her license because she became dependent on prescription drugs after her second husband was murdered. This was a heartbreaker for her, and the result was even more tragic with the previous loss of two of her daughters. One of my sisters was given up for adoption, and the other was taken by the courts. The loss of her nursing license due to the breakdown in mental stamina was only the beginning of many challenges to come. Having had three tragic experiences in her life in relatively close proximity, she then turned to alcohol to ease the pain of defeat. After many years of self-defeating actions, Mother did recover to some degree, but the emotional damage was already done. This was not an easy life for me and my siblings. Throughout our entire lives, in both elementary and high school, we received almost no parental support academically, which in the eyes of a child would appear that what we were doing was not important. Though often hungry and cold, we always had a roof over our heads. This was a hard life for us growing up.

Anyone born into poverty is at a great disadvantage, regardless of where the birthplace may be. Mine is not simply another hard-luck story about lack and losing. My story is about overcoming seemingly insurmountable obstacles, many toils, and many snares. I have come face-to-face with many adversities and demons in my life, and by the grace of God I prevailed. I know all too well about breakthrough and the ups and downs of life. Many individuals experiencing similar circumstances were not as fortunate to overcome. I could have given in to failure or a life of mediocrity, but that was not an option for me, even though the odds were stacked against us as a family.

Additionally, I dealt with the drama of taunts and teasing because my skin was dark. These taunts were not from outside my race, but they came from people who looked like me, people who seemingly had no purpose or understanding of who they were. You see, when I was growing up, having a dark complexion was the basis for a rough life. The saying was then and probably still is now: if you are black, get back; if you are brown, stick around. I've been called every ugly name in the book that would tear most people down: tar baby, little black Sambo, ole black dog, blue Jesus, blacky, and ole black nigga. This type of name-calling, you never forget—and it can forever leave an imprint on your life. Interestingly enough, those who hurled the insults were closest to my complexion. I almost never got this negativity from those who were of truly light complexion. Although I never allowed these experiences to break my spirit, it did take its toll on me. It made me ponder deeply as to why my own people were so cruel in addition to the ongoing cruelty of the white man.

To catch hell from your own people and from the white man at the same time—what a life. But they never broke me down. I kept hearing the words of my mother: "Work and try to have yourself something." I knew I had to break free and make my own way, but growing up in a dysfunctional family, I did not have the right tools and did not know the right people. I've worked my whole life at so many different jobs I can't even begin to name them all. I have run errands for my neighbors, washed dishes at local restaurants, loaded crates of cabbage on big trucks, sacked potatoes out of the fields, and mixed mortar for my uncles who were brickmasons. My brothers, my cousins, and I would even attempt to sell empty whiskey bottles to the moonshiners, and at about age sixteen, I started running a local pool hall, which was a rough place to be. Sixteen, skinny, and black, running an establishment of true cutthroats and headbeaters—one would think I was sure to fail. Most of these guys were older, bigger, and tougher than I was. I thank God I made it out of that place.

I was working, trying to have something, as my mother suggested. I had no plan outside of simply working, and no real mentors to show me the way. I was a below-average student in my school years and had no interest in education at all; I did just enough to get by. I had no real plans and very little hope of being a successful individual. As much as I can remember, the word "success" was never mentioned in my home or my social circle.

The whole idea of success and dreaming became more vivid when I saw my father for the very first time. Tall, good-looking, very well dressed, clean as hospital cotton.

He was talking plenty of trash and driving his new luxury automobile. What an image he had for himself! I remember thinking, "Now that's what I'm talking about." The brother looked like he was handling some things and handling them real well. They called him Cool Breeze in those days. I only saw him four times in my entire life, but I'll give him some credit—his image impacted me more at the time than any other man. He was a bonafide, top-notch hustler, but not a very good father. Deep down inside, I wanted to be and look like him: sharp, witty, self-confident, and successful.

I didn't know at the time I first met my father that he was an underworld figure whose image was the result of ill-gotten gain. He was a high-level drug dealer and a gambling fanatic. Nevertheless, he was an impressive figure and handling lots of cash. What is there not to like about a successful image? He had that in a most magnificent way, more so than any other black man I knew—or white man, for that matter. My mind was set. *I've got to work hard so I can look like my daddy.*

Who can deny that hard work is beneficial? However, there was no vision to go with the purpose, and the purpose was to work and accumulate the trappings of a better life. There was never any talk about saving and not much talk about education. The emphasis was on work—no particular kind, just work. The voice of my mother created in me a certain willingness to do just that, but I had no vision beyond simply working. At a certain point, one comes to realize that there is more to life than simply working and buying homes and cars or whatever new gadget you might like. Work is noble and good, but work without a plan can be very unfulfilling. I discovered I had to develop a plan to fulfill my dreams.

When I started to dream about what I wanted and use my imagination, I realized there was more to life than simply working to gain material things or obtain wealth. It is all right to see yourself as a standout star. If you dare, you can dream. You can live your dream; I am a living witness because I am living mine.

Understanding that there is no barrier that can't be overcome and no challenge beyond your ability to meet is the mindset to have. I have been hungry; almost homeless; sick and without proper medical attention; surrounded at times by killers and crooks; seduced by tricky women and conned by slick brothers; and doubled-crossed, backstabbed, underestimated, and misunderstood by so-called friends. During this time, I seriously began to take a closer look at my life and the consequences of the lives of my so-called friends. I realized that I did not like nor did I want to continue a life that involved criminal and destructive activities. As I examined my life, there were several positive attributes that came to the surface that I did not know I possessed. One was focus, the ability to hone in on what I wanted to achieve and my ability to develop a single minded vision on how to bring it to fruition. The other is the attribute of resolve, to make up my mind not to be denied no matter what may come. I realized that I had the resolve to hold on to my dreams regardless of what the naysayers and mediocre people had to say. I understood that these were powerful attributes. The ability to maintain your focus in the eye of the storm is the key to accomplishment. I had resolve, dogged determination!

It is crucial to keep focused and keep your eyes and your mind on the thing that you want, no matter how dark the night and no matter who doubts you. Do not let anything or anyone get in the way of your dreams. When I made up my mind to change, guess what? Things started to actually change. My breakthrough came in the midseventies after I had been in Atlanta a few years. I realized that my success was my responsibility and not my friends' or my boys'. It was up to me to be something special; otherwise, I would be just another small-time, fake, broke hustler wannabe. I knew plenty of men like this at the time. After all, they say, "Fake it until you make it." I was not interested in fronting as if I had made it. My dream was to live the life that I projected. I wanted to change, and the way to do that is to become the change you see in your mind's eye. The vision or image you have of yourself can, in fact, propel you forward; it can be the catapult that hurls you into the next level of better living. It begins with a vision in the mind. If you can see it in your mind, you can be it in reality. It happened to me.

I walked out on the balcony of my apartment, and suddenly I received a vision. The vision was one where I saw myself speaking to large groups of people from a raised platform. I did not know this would become a reality as it most certainly has. This was not my dream in as much as it was something that came out of nowhere. I believe it was the providence of God. Of course, today I do know where it came from, but at the time it was a passing vision which manifested itself about eleven years later when I started to preach the gospel of Christ. My ministry began in the very same city where I received my initiation into advanced street life and hustling: Atlanta, Georgia. It is the city where dreams come true, and today I am living mine.

Visioning is not an exercise about making money as much as it is an exercise about finding the most powerful and productive you. It is every person's heavenly destiny to become all that God designed them to be. When you are living up to your God-given potential, you will feel at ease and have more clarity. Most people, it appears, do not have a clue about this truth; many are too busy chasing another man's dream. Why not chase your own?

I believe that the providential guiding hand of God protected me through the dangers of yesterday, from my early childhood until the time when I first arrived to the city of Atlanta, Georgia. God foreknew that I would one day do exactly what I'm doing now—crying out to the young and old and letting them know that there is a better way to live and that they can achieve anything their hearts desire.

There were some dangerous times for me, especially during the 1970s and 1980s in the city of Atlanta. Although I tried to maintain a steady income flow and work an ordinary, square job, as the hustlers would call it, I was constantly surrounded by men and women of the underworld. This life kept me looking over my shoulder and asking the question, who can I trust? This was my reality. I was in constant company with lawbreakers and of course, I was a lawbreaker myself, but perhaps not to the extent of some of my contemporaries, some of whom had admitted to me that they had taken other men's lives. My social circle consisted of murderers, check forgers, gamblers, pimps, prostitutes, professional thieves, and high- and low-level drug dealers. Some of them were good people who had made bad choices—certainly not good company, and I was well aware of the ever-present danger, which wore away at my peace of mind. There was no resemblance of a normal life.

I had to break free. I remember very vividly one day I was sitting on a stool in Mama Nelle's soul food restaurant down on Gordon Road (it's called Martin Luther King Boulevard these days). As I sat on that stool eating, depressed and broke, a convict fresh out of the penitentiary struck up a conversation with me, and before long the subject of money came up. He asked me if I wanted to make some, so I responded with a yes; back then I was down for whatever. He began telling me about his idea of robbing a bank; I was listening and still in the game. I had a little moxie back then, plus I was broke and jobless and almost homeless at the time. We started planning the bank robbery. There were about five of us. I only knew one of them slightly before planning this robbery together. His girlfriend was a top-notch booster, a professional thief.

He was a drug dealer along with three others. Each of them had recently lost their connection with their supplier, so we formed this motley crew or band of thieves. A few nights later we went downtown specifically to steal a vehicle to use as a getaway car. We got downtown and spotted a late-model Pontiac. I think the guy had just stepped out and left the motor running to buy a newspaper. When he got back, his car was gone and we had our getaway car. This guy named Johnny was to be the driver, so each day he would run the escape route to and from the bank. The guy who planned the robbery supplied me with a pistol. We all had pieces, guns; however, mine was a little raggedy thirty-eight caliber. Each day for about two weeks we would rehearse our parts, such as what we were supposed to do when we hit the bank door.

Finally, the day had come. We had set up the staging area over near Peyton Road. We had our guns and ski masks ready; we were just about ready to do it. We were parked in one of the newer housing subdivisions, which drew the suspicion of this middle-aged black woman who came down the street and spoke to us. She asked us what we were doing, but no one answered, so she went on to say, "The reason why I asked is because we've been having some break-ins, and when I saw your car and you hanging around, I called the police." When she said that, guys started running to get back in the car, ski masks falling on the ground, pistols dropping, and we made our way out of the subdivision. As we were leaving, we met the police on their way to respond to that lady's call—that did it for me! Before I could rob my first bank, my bank-robbing days were over. Who knows what would've happened if we had been sitting there when the law arrived. Now that is a scary thought because everyone had a gun, and the police for sure had theirs. I had the need to break free of this, or else meet my end at the dark end of a deserted street. This was my life. It may have seemed glamorous, but it was more dangerous than anything—you never knew who to trust. I'd be lying if I did not admit that some parts of this lifestyle were exciting, but counterbalanced with the danger involved, I instinctively knew this kind of living was not for me. The people with whom I associated were smart men and women, but they made their way in life through trickery and slickness, beating the law and anyone else who seemed weak and gullible. Staying away from the police and staying out of jail, or worse, was all a part of the game. Most of the time, these hustlers ended up broke or incarcerated in their old age, if they weren't already dead. Neither one of these was an attractive option for me. Slowly, I began to change my mind, along with the company I kept. Many of the individuals that I knew back then are either dead or beaten up by a lightning-fast lifestyle that consumes the youth of those who dare to play the game. It was a losing proposition then and a losing proposition now. I'm glad I found my purpose and got out.

There is a lot more to my story; however, I'm giving you the condensed version to make a point, which is that when the mind is trained on the right thing in the right way, we are unlimited in what we can accomplish. It was the training of my mind that brought me out. It was right thinking followed by right action. One of the first things I did was to get alone by myself to see who I really was. I knew that if I found the lost, undiscovered me in all of this complexity, then I would possess the power to bring others out. I was a slave to pleasure, excitement, and danger. Some of these desires still taunt me to this day, but with resolve I fight on. Yes, you can become a slave to pleasure and excitement. There are many different types of slavery. If you are going to be liberated, you first have to recognize your bondage. Unfortunately, many of those who are in bondage today do not know that they are slaves. To fear or to be in doubt for no apparent reason can be dangerous and crippling to your emotions.

Remember, you can never conquer what you choose not to confront. It is important to deal with habits such as procrastination, excuses, poor self-esteem, and mediocrity. Allowing yourself to put up with bad company, sorry, nonproductive jobs, or anything that is negative and a barrier to progress can be looked at as a sort of slavery. These barriers and negatives are kinds of demons that must be cast out of your life before you can reap the harvest of plenty and purposed positivity. We will discuss more on this topic later in chapter four.

So, what's the way out? Envision a better you, because that's exactly what I did. I removed myself from the familiar circle of so-called friends and associates. But how could I do this, since most of my years in Atlanta were spent in large circles of unsavory characters—the squares and the hustlers—and that is what I became. However, my time interacting with the schemers and the slick proved to be very informative. There are some valuable lessons to be learned spending time with men and women who make their living by being witty and crafty while evading the police along the way. I had to find a way to break the cycle of mediocrity, crime, violence, womanizing, and night life; it was one party after another, snorting both heroin and cocaine and smoking marijuana almost daily for many years. I longed for a cleaner, quieter life, free from parties and the marijuana smoke. Plus, I did not want to go to jail as many of my associates had done many times. Doing time for crimes you commit was a part of the game of hustling; the true downside of the fast life is the constant thought of jail if you got caught.

How could I make the change to free myself from the madness of the street life? Gambling with my freedom whenever someone came along with a new caper, to make a few fast dollars.

Out of nowhere, the idea of fasting came to mind. In this period of my life, I was heavily influenced by the nation of Islam and talked to some of those brothers about the benefits of fasting. So, desperate for a change, I thought I'd give it a try. This was truly the beginning of my turnaround and the cultivating of a new self-image by way of a new vision of myself. I fasted for the very first time. It was a strange experience. Surprisingly, by the end of the second day, hunger had diminished and was replaced by a sense of accomplishment. During this time of fasting, there was a new and unusual feeling of being on a high. My senses seemed to become more acute as I pursued the challenge to voluntarily give up eating for the purpose of receiving some kind of breakthrough, hoping for my personal epiphany on a quest for a better life.

The search for true purpose had begun. For me, the three-day fast had given a strong sense of accomplishment. I felt strong and ready for new challenges. I went without food on my own, all the while reflecting on the many times in the past I had gone without eating—not by choice, but because I had no money to buy food.

I was beginning to understand the value of self-challenge and goal setting and the power of having a clear-cut, reachable objective.

CHAPTER 2

Understanding the Power of Vision

Since the beginning of time, the world that we live in has been continuously impacted by the ideas and dreams of ordinary people—individuals who looked for a better way to get a task done or a cure for a disease. Set your mind in motion and experience the limitless possibilities of the imagination: the monetary system, railroads, bridges, automobiles, houses, schools, the lightbulb, television, penicillin, blood transfusions, heart transplants, traffic systems, airplanes, space shuttles, music, men walking on the moon, and our modern-day internet system. All of these great advancements came through the imaginations of others. They have impacted human life as we know it. They require the ability to see something mentally that one desires to have and to experience physically. In other words, you can't touch it, and you can't physically see it; however, you can imagine it and dream of it in your mind. Through planning and strategy, it can manifest into reality. Imagination is a most powerful force of the human mind. To see the unseen is an inherited gift from God and serves as a testimony of His glory and power. Through this process, one can learn his true potential and purpose in this world. Unfortunately, few people know how to tap into their own vision to accomplish their life dreams and goals. *Vision Power* is the process of becoming what you see on the inside and bringing into realization the person you really want to be. Step outside of the norm and envision a new mental picture of yourself; one that is a grander, more influential, and a significantly more successful you.

Whatever you want to see yourself doing, whatever you want to see yourself becoming, use your imagination and become what you see. If you don't like what you see, you have the power to change it. It's very much mental.

If you are not pleased with your place in life or your image, you have the power to change it. Within your mind, begin to envision a better you in every aspect of your life. If you can see it on the inside, it can manifest on the outside. This is your time to dream, and you can dream as big and as bold as you please. There are no limitations in your dreams.

Stop selling yourself short. Achievement can be yours; it can fit in your life as well as anyone's. How badly do you want it? It's up to you. You were born to be better in the eye of your mind. Write down all the beautiful things that drift into your mind, whatever they may be. This is not a wish list; this is a get list. Whatever you envision, write it down. Hold the vision of the things you see. Don't be overly concerned with how you're going to reach your objectives.

Just hold your vision, whether it is the building of a new you or a new life. It can be done. When the image of that thing is held, it materializes. This is a law that has been proven time after time. It is a divine principle that works when you know how to use it. This has been referred to as the law of attraction. What do you see for yourself? A new car? See yourself in it, inhale the new car smell. A new home, perhaps? Maybe a certificate of graduation? Envision yourself standing there holding that diploma. Life consists of people's dreams. Whatever you see for yourself in your mind, it can happen.

Dreaming is free and there are no boundaries. What you think about, or imagine for yourself, could be closer than you might think. Prioritizing your desires in the order of their importance gives power and energy to your endeavors. This we will call right thinking.

The powerful point is this: you must see yourself doing or being whatever you desire to be. If it is a Rolex, imagine yourself with it on your arm. See it—what it looks like, feels like. Cut a picture of one out of a magazine and place it in a conspicuous spot so that you can see it every day and position yourself mentally and financially to have it. The mind is a powerful thing. All accomplishments begin in the mind.

When God spoke the worlds into existence, it came out of the inner sanctum of His divine mind. It has been said that what you think about, you bring about. Whatever you want to bring about, you can do with right thinking, right planning, and right patience. It starts with knowing your purpose, and if you know that, this is the foundation and driving force behind the system. Purpose, planning, and patience equals power. Using this system of divine reasoning can unleash the flow of accomplishments and the accompanying prosperity and peace that you hope to gain. Dreams and achievements are only as limited as you dare to dream. See it. Be it. Do you believe in God? If so, remember the word of His son. Mark 9:23: "If thou canst believe all things are possible to him that believeth." And, Mark 10:27: "For with God all things are possible."

It is indeed possible for you to develop this simple but dynamic system of setting and achieving your goals. Let's start right now.

I am convinced that every successful endeavor has to have a certain degree of planning in order to properly manifest. The vision is the compass. It is the lighthouse on the distant shore that allows us to see our way and not dash the ship of our hopes and dreams against the rocks of failure and disappointment.

The vision of the thing we most desire is a beacon of light that continues to keep our destinations illuminated. Any successful endeavor has to have the implementation of a peculiar strategy, whether it is a coach's game plan for winning against an opposing team or a surgeon entering into the most minor procedure. A clearly written and clearly defined vision works the same way. It is first seen in the mind so that the things which are seen through inner vision are not made of things which do appear (Hebrews 11:3). For instance, an architect first envisions a beautiful structure in the imagination. The next step is to put it on paper: the likeness of the building, the working drawings of the building, the specific dimensions, and all the intricate, constituent parts. But at this point, it is not a building. It is what the architect imagined it will look like. Eventually, that which was only a thought, a vision, or a dream, stands to grace the clouds, and it also stands as a testimony to faith and the power of belief. The process transitioned from an idea into the thing imagined, from the intangible idea and vision, to the tangible, touchable reality. There it stands as proof of the power of the vision.

When we dream of better things—a better life, or a higher quality of life—it is imperative that we have clearly defined objectives, including the why and when of what we want, as well as what it is we desire. These objectives and goals must have a timetable for steering. Our vision has a certain magical power when the idea and the image of the thing desired is held in view. One well-known poet by the name of Stevie Wonder referred to this dynamic as "inner vision." The imagination is a mental dynamo, able to crank out the impossible and to deliver into your life the improbable. Use your imagination. It is the untapped power of the ages.

The vision, when clearly defined, is the faith in action. It can be, when used rightly, a fail-safe way to bring about significant changes in a situation, or to bring about change in an individual—even you. It is the right place to begin strategizing and planning for a better life, taking you from the mundane and mediocre to the majestic and marvelous in accomplishments and in quality of life. Life and fullness thereof is a thinking-man's game.

The vision you have of yourself, as well as your hopes and your dreams, form the internal compass that guides you to your destination of choice. It continues as a compass to point to the way that is up. Your own lifestyle can be engineered as much as anything that is made by the hands of a human being. It all starts in the mind, and then manifests openly for all to behold. Whether it is good or evil, it begins with the thought.

The power of vision is more than a concept—it is reality. This allows us to lean on the possibilities of unlimited good and the probability of great discovery because of the unlimited capacity of thought and cosmic energy bringing about the unseen by way of the imagination. This is a doable process that is as real as this present moment. Take a chance on your ability; your own dreams and desires are closer than you think.

Vision Power is about changing lives for the better, facilitating the paradigm shift that will cause you to pause and see your own God-given destiny waiting for you to possess that which has been waiting on you to claim. Habakkuk 2:2 says, "The prophet was told by God to write the vision and make it plain." Begin to see yourself at the next significant level of accomplishment.

Write the vision and make it plain; this is the next-level development that is to be tailored to your strengths and peculiar abilities. It is the designing of a life, your own plan for a better, more dynamic you. Capitalize on the talent and gifts that God placed in you before you were born. You already have the stuff of success. Let's discover its power and potential by visualizing a more dynamic you.

One of the main reasons that there is such a staggering rate of recidivism within our prison system is that those who are constant, repeat offenders do not have a life plan. They have no vision of themselves outside of the criminal activity that keeps landing them behind bars. In order to change your circumstances, you have to change your thinking. If the subconscious mind says crook, convict, or criminal, we can change that by developing a vision of character, charisma, and Christlikeness. The repeat offender has to make the conscious, fervent effort to develop a new image and open himself up to receive the cosmic good, which is in abundance everywhere. But rarely can you find it in abundance in the penitentiary. When the person frees the mind to the unlimited possibilities, then and only then are you able to see the dynamic power of the mind. Many are locked up physically and locked out spiritually and mentally.

The same power of the mind that a lawbreaker uses in his or her effort to do crime can be used in right thinking.

Right thinking brings about right action, and right action brings right results. It is really that simple. This, within the theological realm, is called truth. It's all right to look for the easy way, as long as that way is in accordance to divine law. To the contrary, the right way does not come with the negative baggage that many have to carry when they decide with the conscience mind to break the law of the land.

Vision Power is an adventure, a discovery of self, and the advancing of self-sufficiency by way of the divine mind. Develop and hold a new vision of yourself—a productive, high-achieving, big-thinking, free-to-roam you. See it, seek it, become it. To all my brothers and fathers and sons who have repeatedly graced the prison doors, I say this: when you free your mind, you can free your behind.

For Those Who Do Not Believe

For those who do not believe in a power higher than themselves, this study can still be beneficial. This book will lead you to a more productive place in your life and help you to understand that you have the ability to create your dreams and goals and live a joyful and abundant life. There are countless individuals who have no idea at all as to what their God-given purpose is. They have no dream or chief aim in life and no burning desire to improve the quality of their lives. Millions simply exist in this world, and they are just getting by, watching from the sidelines while others live out their passions and purpose. The *Vision Power* system and strategy will assist in helping you find your true purpose in life. To accomplish this, you must be willing to go to a place that perhaps you have never been before. The challenges you will face are those of self-evaluation. Yes, it can be scary because I am daring you to look at the true cause of your failures, and, most of the time, you will discover it is you. In order to advance to a place of higher productivity, you must be willing to probe the unexplored regions of your mind and look intently into the depths of your personal abilities. You will come to realize that there is an untapped reservoir of vision inside of you, waiting to be stirred up. You will know that it is the gift that has been placed in you by a higher power.

Discovering Your Purpose

Are you willing to step outside of the common and mundane way of doing and thinking and into a new world of possibilities? Determining your God-given purpose could mean traveling in a direction that you have never gone and doing things you have never done. Are you at the place you would like to be in life? Are you accomplishing your dreams and goals? If your answer is no, perhaps you are like many others, doubtful and fearful. Because you are afraid, you have made one excuse after another as to why you have not done better with your life. So, you procrastinate and wait until one day you realize that, in doing so, you have squandered much time. You discover that because of your own laziness or fearfulness, it has cost you many opportunities to get ahead and thrive rather than simply survive. Time is of such value; it cannot be replaced.

Vision Power offers a system that will give you a new hope and allow you to dream bigger and bolder dreams regardless of where you may find yourself right now. The time to stop pretending you have it together and making excuses for being an underachiever is now!

Certainly there will be obstacles to overcome, but I am confident that after you have read *Vision Power* and followed the specific steps in the *Vision Power* system, you will have a better and more refined idea of what your purpose in life is. My hope is that you will immediately begin to live out your dreams and goals with greater fervor and greater faith. Have you ever wondered why so many people scrape and struggle in their attempt to make a living, as opposed to thriving, or why some are wealthy and highly successful while others, even with what we call "decent jobs," can hardly get by? When you discover, through the *Vision Power* system, how to find the real you, true fulfillment will be awaiting. You can live a better life

Others Are Fulfilling
Their Purpose, and So Can You

What do the Mark Zuckerbergs of the world know that you do not? This young man, in his early twenties, is the creator of the phenomenal Facebook social network, which boasts more than 500 million users and counting. Mr. Zuckerberg has become a billionaire and has changed the dynamics of how people communicate online. Do you think that he has discovered his purpose? If he has not, he is certainly off to a mighty good start. Oprah Winfrey is one of the most powerful women in the entertainment industry, and she is a multibillionaire. Is there anyone on the planet who does not know who she is? Oprah has stated during many interviews that she had much fear about leaving Tennessee and moving to Chicago to host the morning talk show; she was a black woman, overweight, and going to a place she knew nothing about, and yet she faced her fears and moved forward. That decision has made her a household name, and she will go down in history for positively inspiring the lives of millions. Sean "P Diddy" Combs is a young recording mogul and multimillionaire who has transformed his musical ability into an empire that includes a clothing line, a fragrance, and a record label that has produced several successful recording artists in the twenty-first century. Sean Combs started out simply as an errand boy, working at a production studio, and made a commitment to himself that he was going to learn all that he could about the music industry. Donald Trump is known for his ability to create a vision and explain it in such a way to others that they invest millions just on his word. He is considered one of the greatest real-estate investors of all time. Some believe he is arrogant and cocky; however, we can't overlook the fact that he is intelligent and savvy in business.

It is undeniable that there is something different about these people. One obvious difference is that they are all wealthy. But these individuals are all transforming and making an impact on how the world is shaped and formed. So can you! Could it be that they have discovered their gifts or purpose, and their wealth is a by-product of them working within their destinies? I know that working within one's area of giftedness can pay great dividends, and you will discover this truth as you find your purpose.

Do not get it twisted; this system is not a get-rich-quick approach, as much as it is an approach to self-development and discovery. By discovering and honing in on your God-given giftedness, you will find your vision and purpose. I take pleasure in saying that *Vision Power* will help you to see your purpose more clearly and guide you in the process. Visioning provides you with the mental and spiritual tools to go where you have never gone and to live a more productive life by way of these time-tested principles. I have heard it said that if you keep doing what you have been doing, you will keep getting what you have been getting. Therefore, if you do not like what you have been getting, you need to change what you have been doing. It's a simple and yet profound truth that speaks to how people refuse to change to see better results.

Living life without a detailed plan will get you nowhere but broke, busted, and disgusted! *Vision Power* is all about providing you with the know-how and tools to determine your life's purpose and develop a detailed plan for your life. Just as no two people's fingerprints are the same, there are other physical and mental distinctions that separate one person from another. With *Vision Power*, you will be able to find and develop your own uniqueness.

It takes a certain amount of courage to be yourself. Joshua, the successor to Moses, was a great soldier whose valor had been displayed on the battlefield. When confronted with the challenge of leading God's people, he showed signs of trepidation and reservation. Here he was, stepping into the shoes of Moses. This had to have been a foreboding experience to envision. In times past, he was an order taker, a follower of the great Moses. Now God was calling on him to lead the entire nation of Israel. Now he was to be an order giver, a leader of many, following the example of Moses. He had seen the example set by his predecessor, but now he had to do it his way. Joshua had to walk now, in his own shoes. The God that he served assured him that he had the resources to do just that. See Joshua 1:6–9 for the success formula. You will find that courage is a principle constituent in being successful and in being your unique self.

Do not be afraid to be you! Many great thinkers and many high achievers have been looked at as being strange—or at least eccentric. The ability to be yourself and find your own track to run on takes courage. After all, when you break from the crowd, there will be those around you who insist that you should remain within the pack. To seek and find one's own purpose takes courage and discipline, and every human being should at least have some of each. Jesus says, "Ask, and it shall be given you; seek, and you shall find; knock, and it shall be opened to you" (Matthew 7:7). To seek out that which gives you fulfillment, and which is in accord with the divine law, is the right place to start as you begin to ask questions of God and of yourself. These questions may include: Who am I? What am I doing on planet earth? Am I doing what I should be doing? Am I in the right place?

This is the right time for sure, and the present time is yours. We each have the same number of hours in a day, both the person of prosperity and the person of poverty alike. Some perhaps spend their days strategically planning with an aim toward success, while others spend it unconsciously planning to fail because they have no plan at all. If you do not have a plan for your life, you are leaving it up to chance. When you know where you want to go, it is easier to get there. Devise a plan to get there instead of walking blindly. The Vision Power system was designed specifically to help you find yourself and your purpose. This system of discovery and enlightenment is not some dark, mysterious secret, but, rather, many undiscovered truths. The wise man Solomon stated, "There is nothing new under the sun" (Ecclesiastes 1:9). I want to share with you discoveries that I and many others have made that can bring some sunshine into your life. While it is true that peace of mind alone is a great accomplishment and that you can have fulfillment in life without monetary wealth, it is also true that you can have both together. For me, peace of mind and being broke do not go together. Believe me, there are very few happy, broke people. Being without the necessities of life is not a happy place to be.

Some are in such a place for lack of life planning and for lack of discovering their true God-given purpose. Poverty can be easily found even if you are not searching for it. The ranks of the poor are swelling daily, even though personal philanthropy is noble, right, and good. Jesus stated that the poor will always be with us. I am a believer in helping those who are in need, those who are poor indeed. The best thing you can do for the poor is to not be one of them!

Be the Best You!

When you find your purpose in life, do not be surprised to find good fortune right alongside it. What a pleasure and rarity it is to find and develop your labor of love. Serve yourself and humanity by laboring within your true purpose in life. In refining your own specialness, do not aspire to be like a particular person, but be your own unique self and discover the richness of individuality. Use the success stories of others to inspire you to find your true Success DNA. It is time for introspection and searching your soul for what makes you tick. Again, one of the most difficult challenges we can ever face is the one of self-evaluation. Tell yourself the truth. Is the profession that you are presently involved in fulfilling? Is it challenging and emotionally inspiring?

I don't know about you, but I have never been pleased with being one of the millions of dissatisfied, bored-to-death, clock-punching masses, or those of the corporate structure and its cutthroat culture of a "kill or be killed" mentality. The corporate system is not designed for your betterment, but for its own financial bottom line. Of course, business is all about profit, but why not use your God-given talent to advance yourself? The sooner you start the search for your own purpose, the happier you will be. Guess what? Quite often you will have to create your own happiness and sense of peace. Your happiness is your responsibility—not your employer's, your family's, your significant other's, or your friends'.

I hope you are in agreement with the importance of discovering your purpose. Gold or diamonds can almost never be found on top of the earth these days. When one is looking for precious metals or gemstones, a lot of digging is required. Not only is it necessary to move tons of earth to get these precious stones or metal, but one has to dig in the right place. Can you imagine the toil and sweat it took to build the railroads that bridged the gap between the East and West Coast? Men suffered and died in order to take part in manifesting someone else's dream of being able to travel from coast to coast. Today, that same rail system allows us to have access to various goods and services in order to sustain our way of life.

Hard work is a mainstay of any worthwhile endeavor, and when you know your purpose, the toil seems like nothing. The Bible records a man by the name of Jacob, who was the second son of Isaac and Rebekah. Jacob struck a deal with his uncle Laban that he would labor seven years to marry his daughter, Rachel. The passage says that Jacob served seven years for Rachel, and it seemed to him but a few days because of the love he had for her. In the end, it was fourteen years before his desire was realized. Hopefully, when you discover what your desire is, it will not take you as long. Knowing day-by-day that you are getting closer to your vision is what makes the journey exciting.

When you are involved in something that you love, the journey to the top is much more rewarding; there is very little toil when your labor is something that brings you joy. Thomas Edison was single-minded, and his vision was one of creating a practical and functional source of light to take mankind out of darkness. Reportedly, Thomas Edison had a great number of attempts and failures before he finally achieved success with the lightbulb. Something so common today came about because of one person who had a purpose and a plan. His dream has been realized many times over. Every time you flick the switch, be reminded of the toil that gave humanity the common, incandescent light source.

CHAPTER 3

Finding Your God-Given Purpose

When you think about finding your life purpose, you might feel overwhelmed, not knowing where to begin your search. Quite often, people associate such terms as "life purpose" with those who are world-renowned for their peace-saving efforts or someone who has saved the lives of thousands or advocated for the rights of people, like Dr. Martin Luther King, Jr. However, it is important for you to know and understand that you do have a life purpose, and in this chapter, I'm going to give you the instructions for finding yours.

For those who are spirit-filled, ultimately your life's purpose is to bring God glory. Each individual on this planet is here for a specific purpose. This is my heartfelt belief. You and I have been blessed with the gift of life—

the great and wonderful experience of this present moment and time. But what is your ultimate aim? What do you do with the precious moments that you have been granted? Do you feel any obligation to make this world a better place by your presence?

Every human being has been created by a sovereign power. The more we recognize and accept this truth, the simpler it is to find one's life purpose. We are here on this earth to make it better through our individual contributions. Are we so naive to think that we, as human beings, are to simply here to live, work, and die? Is that all there is to life?

We did not come into being by chance but by a physiological and biological dynamic. There is a divine reason for every single life. We are not here to become spoilers, liars, losers, murderers, or lawbreakers. When someone begins to operate within the natural order that God designed, that person is then in harmony with God and will automatically prosper in the contribution that he or she makes. This is why it is paramount that each living, breathing human being finds his or her purpose in life. In the grand scheme of things, where do you fit in? What is your role in the great drama of life? Our life's purpose should complement the greater good. The hope is that whatever that is, it will bring meaning and value to the lives of others and to yourself.

Your life's purpose can be as simple as acting upon a deeply rooted positive desire. You must find the resolve to make something good happen in your life. Finding your life purpose will be a journey—one filled with discovery, surprises, and fulfillment. The most important thing to remember is that God has instilled within you the power of talent and potential to achieve anything that you desire to accomplish. You most definitely have a high purpose given to you the moment you had your first heartbeat. From the foundation of the world, the Creator put you here for a purpose. Do you feel your current experiences in life have prevented you from achieving your desires? Do you feel that you are destined to just live a mediocre life? If so, I ask you to set aside your feelings of fear and doubt and be willing to explore the incredible possibilities awaiting you.

Is the Discovery of a Life Purpose Necessary?

While there are people who are content with their lives just as they are, there are others who have a calling to do more with their lives but choose to do nothing. It is my belief that we are all called to do greater things and meet higher challenges. For the most part, humans are not designed to sit still and simply exist. We are miraculously created with the most complex and ingenious mental systems and have the capability to manifest and do great things. However, we all have a choice as to whether or not we will respond and act on our vision, our goals, and our life purpose. If you are reading this book, it means that you are probably seeking something more out of life, and you are looking for the support and answers to make it happen for yourself.

Below are common questions to ask yourself in determining if you are ready to explore your life purpose:

- Have you ever felt like you were supposed to be doing something more than you are doing now?

- Have you had the desire to use your talent and potential to help others?

- Have you had the desire to improve your standard of living?

- Have you ever felt dissatisfied with your job and known you could do better?

- Do you desire to have greater experiences in life?

- Do you desire to help others in a way that can change their lives?

- Do you desire to be a better person, and to contribute more to society?

- Has your daily routine become boring to you?

If you answered yes to any of these questions, then you have already experienced a calling to do more with your life than you are currently doing.

Benefits of Pursuing Your Life's Purpose

As you eventually will learn, your life's purpose will change as you grow and mature in your knowledge of self. Remember in the beginning how I said that it is a journey, and, as such, you are going to change your mind, enhance your purpose, and even reach new levels that you did not even think possible.

Here are some benefits:

- A sense of well-being and satisfaction
- Higher productivity and accomplishment
- Energy and the feeling of excitement
- Contentment and joy of knowing you are fulfilling your purpose

Finding Your Purpose

To start your search for purpose, the first place to look is within. Everything that mankind needs in order to survive and to thrive is within the self. Surprisingly, few individuals have the courage to search the treasure trove of the heart and the subconscious mind.

Your Purpose is something that:

- You feel certain about
- You fit naturally with the thought or concept
- You find joy and love in doing
- You smile just thinking about

Have you noticed that there are certain individuals who seem to have natural abilities to do things that you cannot? Such is the case with singers, dancers, and artists who perform effortlessly with little or no formal training. One of my sons is a naturally good artist, and he appears to have been born with this talent. I have another son and a daughter who are both accomplished singers. Each of them has been given the gift of singing, which is evident upon hearing them, and they have had no formal training. My wife and I both know they were born with it. Famous performers like Mariah Carey, Whitney Houston, Celine Dion, Frank Sinatra, Michael Jackson, Rod Stewart, and Lionel Richie are among the thousands who possess the same gift to a greater or lesser degree. Many have made a very good life out of performing or writing music. There are many others whose singing abilities far surpass those of us who couldn't carry a tune in a bucket. They all do it because they love it; it is fulfilling to them and it comes naturally to them.

There are others who have the gift of science, like Albert Einstein, Louis Pasteur, George Washington Carver—some of the greatest minds of all time. How do you explain the unusual abilities that these men possessed, other than the fact that they were given certain abilities at birth by a higher power? Through hard work and definitive purpose, they achieved greatness. There are also others who have made outstanding achievements because they had a deep desire to gain knowledge through education or nontraditional learning. The point is that some have the aptitude to grasp certain ideas and concepts related to their fields of interest. Therefore, these people are inclined to excel within a particular discipline. Some people create and do great things because they have the desire to do it. Learning a new skill is considerably less rigorous when one has a burning desire to learn within the framework of his or her natural giftedness or intrinsic God-given ability. However, I must admit that even those who don't possess these natural gifts can quite often learn a particular skill if the desire is there.

When you love what you do, your vocation or the service that you render takes on a new meaning. It is no longer defined simply as work—it becomes a joy. The more you enjoy what you do, the more it fulfills you emotionally and, quite often, financially. An example of this truth is revealed among professional athletes. They get paid to play a sport that they love. Some would consider their salaries in many cases to be exorbitant amounts of money; however, these athletes do not seem to mind the lifestyles that their talents afford them.

What Are You Passionate About?

As you begin the journey to discover your life purpose, you will need to dig deep to reveal the golden nuggets waiting for you. Things that you are talented at doing and feel passionate about will often bring joy to you and give you a sense of satisfaction and excitement. On upcoming pages you will find worksheets that contain questions that will help you to begin to brainstorm and search for ideas deep within. There is no right or wrong answer, and you do not have to be long-winded in answering them. Be honest and list what you feel. You may only be able to list a few items in the beginning. Don't give up or give in!

Starting Your Discovery Journey

Now you are ready to start your journey in discovering the first steps toward your purpose. Just as you would prepare for a long-distance trip, you will first need to create a map of how to get to your purpose and establish the resources that you will need to pick up along the way. In other words, you will create a plan by writing down how you will achieve the desires or ideas you have chosen, and you will identify the people, materials, and information you need to make it happen.

It's a good idea at this point to get a binder to keep your ideas in and tab dividers so that you can organize them. Your tab dividers should be labeled:

- **Ideas/Desires**: This section is where you will keep your ideas and plans for how you will implement them.

- **Resources**: This section can be used to keep information on the resources that you will need.

- **Master Calendar**: This section is for your monthly master calendar, where you will set a timeline for accomplishing your goals.

- **Connections**: This section is for names and phone numbers of individuals who can assist you in some way.

- **Miscellaneous Items**: Use this section for keeping items that you need to remember and do not fall within the categories listed above; you can tailor the various sections to your particular needs.

When you get organized and start putting everything together, you will gain a sense of clarity and accomplishment. You will begin to understand why your life purpose is so important.

Designing Your Life Purpose

After you have started planning your life purpose, you might feel a bit overwhelmed and excited about the many choices that you have listed. It also may be challenging to narrow it down to that one thing that you truly want to do. It is at this time that you should pray and meditate on what is the right thing for you. Take your time and read over your list each day. Think back on whether or not you have received compliments from others on the things you have listed. Compliments are great indicators of natural talents. Once you have identified and connected with the one thing that stands out, it is time for you to move forward in listing support or to-do items that will help you to accomplish your purpose. An example of this would be:

- Research required training and education
- Seek out methods to finance your goal
- Hire a coach or identify a mentor
- Modify your personal appearance (attire)

- Establish professional relationships (network)
- Join a professional organization

The above are just a few examples of adjustments you might make in order to prepare yourself for further self-development.

Once you have listed the steps you think it will take to put your purpose into action, simply take one step at a time. For each step, list the tasks associated with accomplishing it. Next, take each task and place it in a time slot in your calendar or planner and stay committed to getting it done. Remember, you do not have to do it alone. There may be a resource or person that can help you to get it done. This is your life, your dream; make it happen. You are as deserving as anyone else to have a life of success and fulfillment. Be patient, be positive, be purposeful.

Remember the Three Ts: Things Take Time

Keep this in mind: whatever you choose to pursue might not be so lucrative. The trade-off might be peace of mind as opposed to financial reward. Finding one's purpose is the ultimate aim. While you may get excited about your newfound discoveries and your purpose, it is not uncommon to start thinking negatively and talking yourself out of taking action on your life purpose. Some common excuses are:

- I've got too much responsibility now to start something else.

- This is all exciting, but I do not have the money to really make this happen.

- I do not want people to think I'm trying to be better than them.

- It's a good thought, but I need to stick with the job I have.

All of the above reasons, and thousands of others, are given each day by those who allow fear to creep in and steal their joy and kill their dreams. Know this beforehand and be prepared and committed to take action anyway. Taking action and moving forward is a sure remedy to procrastination and fear. A few years ago, my wife and I were having dinner with a friend of ours. The conversation was centered on education and various professional work choices. At the time, our friend worked in administration for a large city and probably made a fairly decent salary. As we talked, she admitted that she did not like the work she was presently employed in, even though it paid the bills and helped her to pay for her daughter's college education.

I asked her, "If you could do anything you wanted to do for financial consideration, what would it be?"

She responded, "I really want to be a lawyer; this is my heart's desire."

My next question was, "Why aren't you pursuing your desire?"

Her response was, "I am afraid of failing the LSAT, which is a standardized test that must be passed in order to be accepted into law school."

Well, one thing is certain—with that attitude, she will never know. Unless she confronts her fears, she will never be an attorney. We did our best to encourage her to move forward and conquer her fears. This young woman is not unlike millions of others who are afraid; because of the unknown, they resist the idea of taking action toward their vision or fulfilling their dreams and goals. Many have stopped dreaming or hoping, and they live out their lives vicariously through the achievements of other people. In their minds, it is always the other person who lives in the mansion, the other person who drives the finest cars, and it is always the other person who is saluted or lauded for his or her accomplishments; it is never them. What she needed was a good strong vision of herself as a successful attorney.

Here is some news for you: these same individuals who are high achievers, the ones we admire, who are at the top of their game—they too experience times of fear. So, what's the difference that exists between you and them? They met their fears head on, conquered them, and were victorious—they took action! I have heard some say that they are never afraid of anything, but I don't believe that. Fear can be healthy, but there is also an unhealthy fear. One can propel you forward, and the other can cripple you. Obviously, the crippling fear is the one which has a stifling death grip on those who are slow in the pursuit of their dream. These are the ones who watch from the sidelines as others race toward their destinies to live out their dreams.

The late John H. Johnson, founder of the *Ebony* and *Jet* magazine empire, wrote in his book, *Succeeding Against the Odds,* that he was never quite comfortable in his accomplishments and that he felt as if he was constantly running scared. Perhaps he was attempting to outpace failure. You must both fight your fears and face your fears or you will cower and run. If you run, you will eventually be faced with the same question: why aren't you pursuing your dream?

Proverbs 13:12 of the Holy Bible says this: "Hope deferred makes the heart sick, but when the desire cometh, it is a tree of life." This is so true. When we hope for something over an extended period of time and don't see any progress, or we see only a few signs that suggest that we are not any closer to accomplishing our dream, it causes the shoulders to slump and our steps to drag as we put on the countenance of disappointment and failure, feeling defeated yet again. But how beautiful it is when a long-awaited goal is reached, or when we finally stand on the mountain of accomplishment and say, I made it and look at me now. Deep down inside, everyone wants to win and experience feelings of accomplishment.

The Importance of Discipline

In the 1950s, UCLA coach Henry Russell Sanders made a most profound statement that has been repeated over and over by coaches across the world: "Winning isn't everything; it is the only thing." In order to be victorious in the race of life, you most certainly have to be in it to win it. Tiger Woods, at one time the greatest golfer on the planet, admitted that, when on the course, he is not so much playing to win as much as he is attempting to play his very best game. Tiger Woods's strategy is worth emulating; shouldn't we all attempt to play our best game?

In any field of endeavor, there is the need for discipline. Without discipline, you are missing a vital component in the foundational structure of accomplishment. Discipline, quite frankly, is the will to do what you don't want to do when you know you must do it in order to reach beyond the norm. If you want life to be easy on you, you have to be hard on yourself. People who are very successful at what they do are willing to do what others are not. This takes discipline, drive, tenacity, and the burning desire to get that which you have never had. The desires that you have will not always show up. You'll have to find them. Finding and understanding your purpose can be a grueling and arduous task, but well worth it in the end.

There are often things that are blocking our way as we move toward our destinies. These obstacles are not always easy to spot. We will refer to these barriers as demons; these demons must be identified and eradicated. They are in the path of your good, and they must be removed; they are blocking the view of the new and better you. The following chapter is entirely dedicated to identifying and eliminating the vision blockers in your life. They are the habits and practices—physical, mental, and otherwise—which have been hindering you from seeing and becoming a better you. This is an exercise in finding out what makes you tick. Who are you really? Why aren't you more accomplished, and why isn't your life more celebrated?

CHAPTER 4

Eliminating the D.E.M.O.N.S.

If you live long enough, you will have challenges and obstacles in your life that prevent you from truly carrying out your vision. I certainly have had my fair share of these obstacles—so much that I gave them a name. I call them D.E.M.O.N.S. (demons), and while you might first think of imps of the devil, these demons all have to do with poor habits and the lack of action that prevents us from achieving our heart's desire.

D.E.M.O.N.S.

D = Distractions

E = Embedded

M = Mentally

O = Obscuring

N = New

S = Self

Demons can prevent you from achieving your goals and thinking positively about yourself and others. They can keep you buried under piles of emotional negativity, deferred dreams, unmet expectations, and hobbled hopes. This is why it is so very necessary to rid yourself of them. Once you do, you can develop the new productive, positive, progressive, and purposeful you!

Below, I've identified eight demons that can truly wreak havoc on your life if you allow them. Just as the acronym states, they can distract you by embedding themselves so deeply in your subconscious mind that they can obscure any hope of you creating a new self. These eight demons are:

1. **Doubt**

2. **Fear**

3. **Bad Habits**

4. **Excuses**

5. **Procrastination**

6. **Distraction**

7. **Guilt**

8. **Negative Relationships**

I am sure there are many other demons not mentioned, but the list above represents some of the common challenges that have disrupted the lives of so many people—

and perhaps even yours. These are roadblocks and clutter, obstructions in your way that surround you. One or all could be standing in your way right now and not allowing you to clearly see the real person God intended for you to be. You must locate and eradicate these demons and rid yourself of each, one by one. You must clean your house, which is your inner conscience, of the clutter of negative self-perception. There is something getting in your way. What is it? Why is it? How can you get around the obstacles that cloud your view of a glowing new and better you?

There is a parable given in the Gospel of Luke about a woman who had ten pieces of silver and lost one piece (Luke 15:8). She proceeded to sweep the house, and looked diligently until she found it. This parable in principle is speaking to the value placed in that one coin. There is a vivid point in this account that we must grasp, and it is that she cleaned up the house as she looked for the silver. The time is now for you to begin to sweep the inner sanctum of your soul in searching out your true purpose in this life. Which of these inner demons is plaguing you and keeping you from a more dynamic self? Which ones are holding you back from fulfilling your dreams? You must develop the resolve to not let anything or anyone get in the way of you fulfilling your vision of a new and better you. The word that breaks the spell of these psychological misfits and dream-blocking invaders is the word "resolve." Say this now and say it out loud: "I resolve to not let anything or anyone get in the way of my God-ordained good, laid aside for me since the foundation of the world."

Demons of Doubt and Fear

"If ye have faith and doubt not . . . ye shall ask in prayer, believing, ye shall receive" (Matthew 21:21–22). The demons of doubt and fear, for instance, have been the slayer of many a dream. They have been the saboteur of noble pursuits and grand visions of the hearts of countless men and women who dared to look beyond the ordinary and into the treasures of endless possibilities. Doubt, as defined in the ancient biblical text, is to be without resource to judge diversely; having a conflicted mindset based upon lack of information or lack of resources, thereby inhibiting progress. Therefore, the more information that one has about the thing that he doubts, the more likely he is to overcome the feelings of uncertainty. Doubt is a choice you make, and, quite often, it is based upon a perceived negative outcome. Thoughts of doubt and fear eat away at our faith, and the more one's faith is attacked, the bigger and bolder doubt and fear become. Doubt and fear often succeed in convincing the visionary that the things they dream of can't be done. Remember, if it is envisioned within the scope of your mind and within the will of God, it can be done! If it is noble or needed, it can be done. Therefore, you must affirm that doubt and fear are liars and deceivers.

A very important point to remember is that doubt and faith cannot live peacefully in the same house. "And if a house be divided against itself, that house cannot stand" (Mark 3:25). In addition, faith and fear do not harmonize, and doubt is only fear wrapped up in a different package. Both are only there to hinder your progress, and one of them is rarely seen without the company of the other. These demons are bad company in the life of someone who is attempting to be a better person and live life to the fullest. Resolve is the key in eliminating doubt and fear. Positive and unwavering faith in light of truth cancels out darkness and destructive doubt. One of the biblical definitions for doubt is to be without any resources. As a believer in almighty God, I believe without reservation that I serve a God who has everything I need in infinite supply. The demon of doubt, which plagues the minds of many, is uncertainty of belief, which often interferes with decision making. It is a deliberate suspension of judgment; it is to be lacking in confidence and conviction. Doubt will take you nowhere real fast. In the words of

Ralph Waldo Emerson, "The world makes way for the man who knows where he is going."

Do you know where you are going? If the answer is, "I don't know," you are still headed somewhere, but you don't have the control over where you're going. If you do not know where you are going, you could very well end up in a place most uncomfortable and on the deficit side of life. Diana Ross, one of the greatest vocalists of our time, asked this in one of her many hit tunes, "Do you know where you're going to? Do you like the things that life is showing you?" If you don't like what life is showing you, you can make a change.

Doubt is removed by resolve. The constant doubter can't make up his mind with conviction; he takes one step forward and two steps backward in his approach to life and the many challenges that it brings. He ends up on the deficit side of things and circumstances. The spiritual message is this: "But let him ask in faith, with no doubting, for he who doubts is like a wave of the sea driven and tossed by the wind. For let not that man suppose that he will receive anything from the Lord; he is a double-minded man, unstable in all his ways" (James 1:6–8). This passage describes a person who is experiencing great uncertainty.

The problem of uncertainty comes from our personal past experiences and failures. Certain disappointment and the pain of it all tends to make us somewhat apprehensive about the future. The surest way to avoid repeating this pain or disappointment is to not try that particular task again. How do you overcome this? Just gather yourself and try it again and again. At least you know now what does not work, based upon yesterday's failure. Why sit by and simply watch as someone else lives their dream? Winners never quit and quitters never win. Life truly is not a spectator sport. Forget about how many times you might have failed or the idea that what you want to do has never been done before. So what—you be the first! Remember there is always a first. Why not you? Keep this in mind also—every person on earth has some doubt about something. Don't be paralyzed by it; get into life! If you don't live your own life to the fullest, no one can do it for you. You be the star of your own show. Each of us has a role to play in the great drama of life.

You can be a star or an extra. It's your choice. You be the victor of your own battles. Be your own hero. Be the best you, because that is what life is all about. Stop attempting to get fulfillment by way of someone else's accomplishments.

In the autobiography of sports great Deion Sanders— *Power, Money and Sex*—he mentions the thing of which he was most afraid. Had he not thrown himself headlong into being the best ball player he could be, he could have

ended up being an "if ida" —meaning "if I would have" —
in his old age. There are many people in the "if ida" club
today! You know the people that say: if ida tried harder,
I could have; if ida finished my studies, I would have; if
ida followed the right plan, I could have. Woulda. Shoulda.
Coulda. If you don't stop doubting yourself, this is where
you'll be, joining the throngs of talkers and dreamers, never
really getting there because you gave up too soon. You've
seen it, or heard it, time and time again. They are the fellas
long past the flower of their youth who sit around talking
about what they could have done and should have done,
but time has passed them by. The clock for achievement has
run out; the buzzer has sounded, and the game is all but
over. The chance at greatness has been lost and all they have
now are stories of yesterday about what they could have
done —what a waste. If time is creeping up on you, and
you've been dreaming, talking, and procrastinating, before
you know it, you will also be in the "if ida" club! Make up
your mind that you are getting back in the game and, come
hell or high water, you're going to get your good. Weigh
the facts, gather the data, and go for it. Resolve to move
forward, and doubt be damned! Resolve will always trump
reservation. Resolve is the demon slayer of doubt.

Doubt and fear are certainly connected; either they
are satanic siblings or demonic first cousins, but they are

connected just the same. They are stumbling blocks in your way—pesky little imps who hound your self-conscience, eat away at your confidence, block your progress, and keep you from your God-ordained destiny. Technically, fear is an emotional response to a perceived threat. It is a basic survival mechanism occurring in response to a specific stimulus, such as pain or the thought of pain, whether physical or emotional. Pain is pain, and no one wants an ongoing relationship with it.

There are expressions that we have heard during our lives, like heartbroken, heartsick, or the blues. This pain deals with the emotions, and many feel that this type of pain is as severe as the physical type. For example, some people would rather not get involved with another for fear of being hurt emotionally, or perhaps others refuse to take even a calculated risk to get ahead in life because of the emotional setback that could occur in the event of failure. This kind of unjustified fear is stifling and nonproductive; it is a life-wrecking and dream-stealing emotion. It is of no value at all, and it places you farther behind in your hopes and expectations for yourself and those you love.

During a dark time in our country's history, Franklin Delano Roosevelt, the thirty-second president of the United States, summoned the power of God and his own intestinal fortitude and stated that "the only thing we have to fear is fear itself." With this mind-set and this positivity, he led America into a new day, giving the nation hope where there perhaps was little hope at all. He moved forward, leading the nation with a combination of optimism and action. Fear is the nameless, unreasoning, unjustified terror which paralyzes needed efforts from moving forward. The boogeyman is not real; he is a figment of your imagination. Maybe you didn't shake him or get over him as a child, and you unconsciously brought him into adulthood, having hidden him away in the dark recesses of your psyche. Suffice it to say, most of our fears are unwarranted, unjustified, and unreal. Take a good, hard look at yourself and ask these questions: What am I afraid of? I want to move forward and upward—what's stopping me?

Replacing Doubt and Fear with Courage and Faith

Below are affirmations to be repeated throughout your day if you are dealing with the demons of doubt and fear. Positive repetitive thoughts can help you work through negative thoughts and reinforce your desire to fulfill your vision.

Affirmation #1

"I see myself as fearless and full of faith. I will not allow fear or doubt to keep me from my good and from my divine, God-ordained destiny."

Affirmation #2

"I am only limited to the size of my dreams and the scope of my vision. My dreams are bigger than my doubts and greater than my fears."

Demon of Bad Habits

When your demons are bad habits, you must first determine what those bad habits are and eradicate them the same way as you would doubt and fear. As you search your mind and heart, be honest with yourself about your own continued involvement in activities or behaviors that would fit this category. Consider the pain associated with persisting in things that are counterproductive. Just because it brings you relief or comfort doesn't mean that it is a good practice. It simply brings you temporary relief; therefore, these bad habits are repeated consistently. Because you're comfortable and do not fear these behaviors, you continue the pattern. However, if a habit prevents you from achieving your vision or reaching your goals, it's a habit you need to eliminate. Replace the demons of bad habits with the spirit of good habits.

Every negative and counterproductive practice we engage in can be replaced or supplanted with a positive one. The same way we pick up bad behavior, we can unlearn that behavior that which works against us and begin new productive behaviors that work for us in a positive more life enriching way. This all boils down to how much you value your life and wellbeing. I suppose that most of us have some bad habits, to some degree. However, to attempt to replace destructive practices with constructive practices is at least common sense.

Demon of Excuses

Another destructive dream killer, robber of productivity, and a spoiler of advancement is the demon of excuses. Is it really as simple as *just do it*? Well, the only way to get the task done is to get it done. Just do it—the quicker you get to it, the closer you get to your reward. Let me give you an example. I don't like going to the gym to work out, although it's healthy and stimulating for my body. I don't like the atmosphere because it can be distracting. It's easy for me to find a reason not to go, such as "I got up too late, so I won't go today," or "I'm too tired to go today." Whatever the reason may be, I still know it is the right thing to do. The good coming out of it greatly outweighs the grind of it all. In the end, the excuse can simply be a need for inspiration. We all need some encouragement sometimes. We need it and we should give it. The more excuses you make for not performing a necessary task, the deeper in the hole of underachievement you go. Quite often you have to inspire yourself. Don't let the demon of excuses keep you from your good.

Perhaps while reading this you are wrestling with these very demons, and they are getting in your way. If so, you're probably feeling that your life is slipping away minute by minute. You are dealing with one of the deadliest demons because it is silent and subtle. It quietly eats up your time until one day all your good time has been used up. These demons, like all the others, must be eradicated, because as long as you keep coming up with one excuse after the other, you are digging deeper into the hole of "do nothing." You're standing on the sideline watching others win the awards. How fulfilling is it, thumbing through glossy magazine photos of your favorite celebrities, who have done what you didn't have the discipline to do. So, you pine away living vicariously through someone you don't even know. In your own mind, you want the same thing, but lack the knowledge and drive to get there. Don't give up on your own dream. Stop with the excuses. Start planning to get yours too. Excuses—what a dream robber, what a killer of success. What a dirty demon.

Affirmation #1

"No more excuses for not getting the important things done."

Affirmation #2

"Whatever is important, I'm going to get it done now. If not sooner, I shall find a way."

Affirmation #3

"From this point forward, I excuse myself from excuses blocking my blessings."

Demon of Distraction

Distraction is defined as that which turns one aside, diverting the attention to a different object or a different direction. It can stir up or confuse you with its conflicting emotions. Therefore, I will refer to this as a deceptive demon because it has the power to mislead and cause you to believe an untruth. Whatever gets in the way of your objective can be an untruth. For example, distractions can be a friend, relationship, your environment, a personal hobby, and even television. If your actions are not contributing to your dreams and goals, they could be hurting you. Maybe you don't feel the pain yet, but it's coming.

Distractions are as numerous as the sands of the seashore. Whatever it is that interferes with your main focus could very well be a distraction. Whatever or whoever it is, if it's not helping you toward your destiny, it's moving you away from your destiny. Again, if it's not working for you, it's working against you. It is something that comes seemingly out of nowhere to ambush or side-track you from your main focus. Something as simple as a recreational pastime that you might use as a hobby, if not contained, can become a distraction. Countless hours browsing the Internet is a widespread curiosity that quite often bears no fruit at all. According to interruption scientist Gloria Mark, "The average worker switches tasks every three minutes, and once distracted, a worker takes nearly thirty minutes to resume the original task, thereby lowering the productivity of that individual." It does appear that distractions are major causes of procrastination. Distraction is the inability to identify, attend to, or attain what is valuable, even when we are hardworking or content. Developing the power of concentration is the key component in overcoming the insidiousness of this particular demon. Keep your focus on the task, even in the midst of abrupt interruptions that come into view out of nowhere, no matter the type of disruption it might be. It has been said that a distraction is a "fake target," which is often used in warfare to expose the enemy's weaknesses. Distractions are mental intrusions that snatch away the intended focus from one task and, by craft, force your attention to the distraction of another.

Preoccupation with comparing yourself to other people is a sure sign of this heinous demon. Attempting to measure your sense of self-worth by the accomplishments of others is destructive and can be deadly. You can only be the best you and build your own intrinsic talents and abilities. Don't use your valuable time trying to be a duplicate of someone else.

Another distraction is when you allow yourself to get caught in activities that are nonproductive. For example, a young man, unemployed, sits at home all day long playing video games. When he finishes, he masters the game and wins, but when it is all said and done, he is still jobless and broke. His only consolation is that he is even more proficient at the video game.

For the sake of simplicity, let's call distraction an illegitimate, ill-timed excuse embroidered into the tapestry of fruitless idleness.

If the average television viewer watches five hours of television per day, at the end of a calendar year, that person would have watched about seventy-six whole days of programming. Startling, isn't it? Statistics state that the average American watches at least five hours of television per night. Therefore, if that same person continues that trend over a fifty-year period, they will have spent over ten whole years looking at the tube. It is remarkable how much time we spend watching other people's lives. How much entertainment do you really need? Remember, the demon of procrastination feeds off of the demon of distraction. Too much television is a huge distraction, unless watching television is your means to a financial end.

It's like sitting in a rocking chair, going back and forth; you are moving, but, in reality, you are not going anywhere. One young educator I interviewed put it like this when I asked her to define distraction in her own words: "Distraction is when things get in the way." While watching television can have an educational value, conversely, it is known to be one of the greatest wasters of time. For many people, it gets in their way for hours at a time. I must admit that staying on task is not always so simple to do. Become aware of the things that are getting in your way. For some, it's TV, but for others it might be something else. Many of us have some ongoing distractions that interfere with our productivity, and these distractions, whatever they may be, are like invisible saboteurs working in the background, blocking the way to your good.

Demon of Procrastination

Procrastination is the act of delaying or putting off something that you're purposed to do. This time frame of putting off can spiral out of control and last for days, weeks, months, years, and for some, even a lifetime. There are many older people today who have a life of regret all because they procrastinated in taking action on their visions, dreams, and goals. Often, procrastination can result in a backlash of negative consequences. For example, many people know that they should maintain their books and prepare for paying their taxes before the deadline. However, should they choose to procrastinate, they will surely experience the pain of having to pay a late fee, penalties, and interest, all because it was too painful or overwhelming to them to have their taxes prepared. You must also be careful of rationalizing or talking yourself into putting things off. This is a common form of making it okay to procrastinate. A simple rule is to make a commitment to take action and start the project or task you must do as scheduled. A key to overcoming this is focus. Develop the practice of doing the important things sooner rather than later. Make it a habit to take care of business immediately, if not sooner. The desire to procrastinate is simply a bad habit that can have devastating consequences if not dealt with. Change your mind and change your state. Start to function highly in getting the task at hand completed. Procrastination is, in its essence, an excuse wrapped up in the packaging of a lie disguised as the truth.

The demon that seemed to have had a fierce attachment to me was the demon of procrastination. Yes, I discovered that I had a chronic case of "last-minute-itis" and "do-it-later-itis." I finally looked up one day and found that I had wasted much of the time given to me, which is the most valuable resource we all possess. I resolved never to waste such a precious gift, and I work hard at eliminating procrastination daily. It has been said that time is a master worker that heals the wounds of temporary defeat, equalizes the inequalities, and rights the wrongs of the world. There is nothing impossible with time. Therefore, we must attempt to use every second with as much productivity as possible.

Demon of Guilt

Guilt, in the world of psychology, is defined as an unpleasant feeling associated with unfulfilled wishes — a sort of self-imposed punishment for not performing a particular task that was in your power to perform. There are different types of guilt. Survivor's guilt, for instance, is when a person is the only one to survive some kind of catastrophe. It is also a cognitive or emotional experience that occurs when a person realizes or believes, accurately or not, that he or she has violated a known moral standard and bears significant responsibility for that violation. Biblically, guilt is not merely an emotional state, but also a legal state of deserving punishment for having violated the law of God. This is reflective of the weight and the guilt Cain bore for murdering his own brother. "And Cain said unto the LORD, my punishment is greater than I can bear" (Genesis 4:13).

When Judas betrayed Jesus Christ, the weight of it all and the ensuing feelings of guilt were too much for him. He could not live with himself after spilling innocent blood, a gross violation of the highest kind. He could not shake the thought of what he had done; therefore, he committed suicide (Matthew 27:5). Here was the manifestation of guilt and the immense weight of having violated one's conscience, and, more pointedly, taking another person's life—not just any life, but the life of the Son of God.

The demon of guilt can be incurred in a plethora of ways. It must be dealt with and eradicated like all the other demons in order for you to set the proper vision for yourself after you have determined your true purpose in life. Guilt is another deadly demon, and in this book, we will address the ways in which you can move beyond this stifling condition to identify your purpose and map out your vision.

Demon of Negative Relationships

How many dreams have been dashed against the rocks of negative relationships? This particular demon embraces a wide range of relations, including husbands, wives, children, in-laws, friends, and of course, enemies. Employees as well as employers can also all fall within these groupings. Anywhere you find toxic thinking that tends to aggravate, irritate, or bad-mouth your dreams and work against your purpose, knowingly or unknowingly—these are saboteurs of your good. Those who you hold most dear now could be the very ones you might have to leave behind as you advance toward your destiny. You must admit that some of the individuals in your circle are simply not good for your emotional or spiritual health. Some of these people could be the quintessential dream killers, haters, or envious and small-thinking people that want to hold you back. Since these individuals have not advanced, it is difficult for them to watch as you move to a higher place of achievement. A classic case of a dream-killing relationship is the one of Joseph and his brothers, in the book of Genesis. The jealousy and bitterness toward him from his brothers started when their father, Jacob, gave Joseph a coat of many colors (Genesis 37:3). Jacob favored Joseph over his siblings. His brothers began to hate Joseph, and the conspiracy to get rid of him was born. Joseph's dream exacerbated the problem even more. His dream indicated that one day he would reign over the entire family. In this case, the negative relationship was in Joseph's own family.

"And a man's foes shall be they of his household" (Matthew 10:36). There are cases when the most negative and caustic relationships are those within our immediate circle— even in your own home. We must be careful about the circle of friends or associates we choose and the environments that we place ourselves in. Association begets assimilation, and assimilation begets similarities. In other words, those in your circle can influence and/or corrupt your thinking.

The Search for Light in a Dark, Quiet Room

Now that you know what the acronym D.E.M.O.N.S. means, and you've been introduced to the eight demons that can hold you back, it's time to get rid of them! I want to share with you a technique I have been using for years that has helped me and others I have shared it with. I call it "The Search for Light in a Dark, Quiet Room." It's time to explore the unexplored in your mind; it's time for you to experience solitude. It's time to seek and dig in your own gold mine and discover the gold of your heart. There are so many people living life on the surface every day. Perhaps they have neglected to dig beneath the surface and go to that dark, quiet place where, ironically, light can be discovered. I'm talking about the light of self-discovery, purpose, destiny, and vision coming face-to-face with your inner self. Perhaps many don't like to think too deeply, or address how they are feeling, or even ask themselves why they are feeling so low or what their life purpose is. However, it's thinking deeply and being committed to discovering your true self that will set you free to truly reach your potential and carry out your vision!

Why a dark, quiet room? In an attempt to center yourself and to search the inner sanctum of your soul, you need a place that is free from distraction, free from the noise of the outside, in order to confront your inner demons and imps. It's interesting that to develop a negative film into the positive print, the room must be dark in order for the photographer to go through the process of bringing to light the images as seen through the lens of the camera. In the same way, we must go into this dark, quiet room where there are no distractions to interfere with the conscious mind. When you are not able to look without, you are forced to look within. Here you are alone, and to be alone is to be reminded of who and what you really are. For many of us, this can be a frightening and eye-opening experience. Brigitte Bardot, a beautiful and famous French actress during the 1950s through 1960s, had this to say about solitude: "Solitude scares me; it makes me think about love, death and war. I need distraction from anxious black thoughts." This woman, in her sincere honesty, has worded the thoughts of many people. However, it is in solitude that great discoveries can be made. In your case, the plan is for you to discover the real you. In particular, it is to locate and eradicate the demon that is blocking your progress. Remember, you can never be your best you until you do serious self-evaluation.

It is time right now to look deep within your own soul and ask the hard question as to what it is that is holding you back from realizing your dream. This is not about challenging circumstances or so-called disadvantages you might perceive. This is all about you and your true shortcomings, which are the demons you must seek out and eradicate. They are barriers that must be overcome; whatever it may take, let's get it done!

This dark, quiet room experience is a quest to get past every excuse you have ever made as to why you are not where you want to be. I have no idea what your demons look like, but whatever they are, they are in your way! It's up to you to do something about them, or you can continue to live life vicariously through others. You can resolve right here and right now to stop looking at life and start to live it, enjoy it, and thrive while doing it.

The answers we seek and the truth we seek about ourselves can often be discovered in solitude. Absolute alone time can be both revelatory and refreshing. In order to move forward with your hopes and dreams, it is imperative that you discover what it is that stands in the way of your better life. Schedule some time when you know you'll be alone at home or wherever you feel comfortable to search for your light. This exercise is designed for you to take a deep and honest look at yourself. In a dark, quiet place, search your heart and soul for the obstacles that have been a barrier to your progress. You are facing the music, as they say, doing something uncomfortable and unusable in an attempt to find the culprit—the demon that's been hanging you up. Cut off all electronics, including your cell phone. Next, go in a room that is comfortable to you. You can sit in a chair or in a comfortable position on the floor. Turn all lights off. Pull the shades down or close the blinds. The goal is to have the room completely dark. Darkness can automatically bring about an uncomfortable feeling, so be prepared to possibly feel uneasy. Sit in your prepared space, close your eyes, and relax. Begin to ask yourself questions, such as: What's holding me back from accomplishing my dreams? What do I want out of life? What am I unhappy about? Do I love myself? What demons are obscuring the new me? Ask the probing questions of yourself. Wait for the answers—they will come. You might not like what you get, but be honest with yourself. This is a search for the truth, and in this dark, quiet room you will surely make some discoveries.

The goal of this exercise is to confront the things that are blocking your path, whatever they are. They could be one of the eight D.E.M.O.N.S. mentioned or something else that you have identified. Whatever the case, confront them and conquer them! You'll have all kinds of thoughts going through your mind; however, keep moving forward and allow them to come up to the surface.

After the exercise, turn on the lights, get your notepad out, and start writing down the questions, answers, and thoughts that entered your mind. Schedule frequent sessions of doing this exercise; as you increase the time frame between each session, answers and ideas will come to you, and you'll begin to get in touch with the real you. Remember, it's okay to feel uneasy or experience some anxiety. Remember, sometimes you have to do something out of the ordinary in order to progress in life. If you want something you never had, you might have to do something you have never done. Try this exercise on for size. You have nothing to lose but the habits and hangups that have been holding you back.

Finding the new you, your purpose, and your vision can be done. Make note of the things that are blocking your way. When you discover what is in your way, you will be on your way, setting goals and establishing bolder visions for the future. When you begin to identify these obstacles, seek also solutions as to how you can begin the eradication process of these weaknesses. Have courage!

CHAPTER 5

Eight Steps to Writing Your Vision

"Write the vision and make it plain."
Habakkuk 2:2

As discussed in chapter two, vision is the ability to see something that one desires and to experience that which is otherwise internal and not yet tangible. The power in visioning is when you actually take the thought process and transfer it plainly on paper for planning and implementation. This is the first step toward manifesting your dreams, and often the step that is missing for many people, which is why they don't realize their visions. In addition to having the passion to carry out your vision, you must also have a strong commitment and will to see it through. You are in complete control of your life's hopes, and you have the power to speed it up or slow it down. With that said, it's now time for you to focus on writing your vision and making it plain. My goal for writing this chapter separately is for you to have the knowledge from the previous chapters in order to better understand the importance of the planning stage of reaching your objectives.

The first thing you should do right now is ask yourself the question, "What are the demons that can hold me back from implementing my vision?" Hopefully, you should have identified your demons by completing the exercise in the previous chapter. If not, I suggest you go back and complete the exercise so you can come face-to-face with those demons that are holding you back. For many, just scheduling the time and actually putting pen to paper seems to be a problem. Just remember that you are in control and that it's not important that you write a novel, manuscript, or workbook. You just need to gather your ideas, such as in a bulleted list or short paragraphs, to help you organize your thoughts. My prayer is that you will allow the process of visioning to transform your life into something even more amazing than it already is, and that you realize you are worthy and already possess the power, talent, and potential to accomplish great things.

Parts of a Vision

There are six basic areas you should consider when writing your vision statement. It will be important to write at least one goal you would like to accomplish for each of the following areas:

- **Education/Learning**

  Are there any experiences that you would like to have in this area, such as going back to college, getting a certification, or taking a workshop?

- **Family/Friends**

  Are there any relationships that you would like to improve upon, renew, or add to your social circle?

- **Health**

  Are there any considerations you have in improving your health (e.g., losing weight, exercising, or altering your diet)?

- **Financial**

  Where are you financially? Would you like to stabilize or improve your financial position? For example, do you want to get out of debt or start a savings account?

- **Spiritual**

  What would you like to experience in your relationship with God (e.g., greater intimacy or greater knowledge)? Do you want to develop a higher level of spiritual maturity?

- **Career**

  Have you considered embarking upon a new career, starting a business, or commencing some other fulfilling endeavor?

These are just a few of the things one might contemplate when writing your vision. By exercising your vision power and utilizing the processes you have read in this book, you can reach your potential and objectives.

Getting Started

Step One: Eliminate Distractions

Schedule some time in your day for at least the next three to four weeks (thirty minutes each day). Make sure you're in a quiet and personal space where you will not have any distractions. Adjust the time as much as you need to write your plan.

Step Two: Brainstorming

Based on what you've read in the *Vision Power* text and the exercises and worksheets I've provided, start brainstorming and ask yourself questions regarding what you think your vision is.

- What am I most passionate about?
- What touches my heart?
- What places do I want to see in the world?
- If I could change the conditions or lives of others for the better, what would it be?
- What am I inspired to do?
- What do I do so much that I forget to eat or sleep?
- What education or knowledge do I need?
- How is my health?
- What is my relationship with God?
- What type of career do I want?
- What are my financial needs?
- Am I entrepreneurial?

Once you've answered these questions, start writing your personal vision statement. Try writing in first person, and don't worry about being too long in the beginning. The most important thing is to get something down on paper.

The sky is the limit, so don't put any limitations on yourself, your time, your money, or your vision. It may take some time to truly dig down and get your thoughts flowing. However, you must move forward and not allow the demon of procrastination to get in your way—right? Of course!

Additional Questions to Consider:

- What would you like for others to say about you—in this present time, or when you are gone?

- What would you like to be known for?

- How do you want your family, friends, associates, and others to remember you?

- At the end of your life, what would matter most to you?

- What would you regret not having done or accomplished?

Step Three: Write a One Sentence Vision Statement

Next, try to write your vision in one sentence (for example, my vision is to inspire young men and women to a greater good):

_____

_____

_____

_____

Step Four: Identify Challenges You Might Face

Challenges are a part of life, and they can be very complex and get in the way of accomplishing your vision. It is probable that, when you start writing your objectives, the demons of fear and doubt can set in and you will begin to waiver while implementing your plan. To prevent this from happening to you, write down any challenges or thoughts that you feel could hold you back or distract you from staying focused on your vision. Next, write down the solutions to your challenges.

Take your time—it's okay if you don't have immediate answers for it. The point is to be prepared and on the lookout for demons that creep up. (See list below.)

D.E.M.O.N.S.

D = Distractions

E = Embedded

M = Mentally

O = Obscuring

N = New

S = Self

Identify Knowledge and Resources Needed

Now that you've got your first vision statement written, it's important to know what information and resources you'll need to support your vision. For example, if you plan on starting a business, do you need to take a business start-up workshop, and do you have enough capital? If you plan on going back to school, do you need to figure out how you will secure financing? Are you working a full-time job that is presenting a time challenge? Do you need to find childcare or figure out how you'll find the funds to pay for it?

Next to each area of your vision, make sure you list the knowledge and resources you'll need to bring your vision forth.

Step Five: Write Down Goals to Support Your Vision

Goals are the catalysts for manifestation. Just imagine your vision is formed in your mind, then you'll take that thought and transfer it out of your mind and onto paper.

Next, you're identifying the actions you'll need to take in order to manifest that goal, so you can see, feel, experience, or touch it—it's one powerful technique!

Write down the goals you feel are necessary to carry out your vision. Next to each goal, list a time frame that you would like to accomplish it. Remember, goals are specific and straight to the point. Their job is to truly support the vision and make it happen, so there's no need to be too wordy.

Step Six: Create Your Circle of Success

While you are the one that is responsible for being the leader of your vision, it doesn't mean that you have to do it alone or be by yourself. Make a list of talented and knowledgeable people that would not only be supportive, but are positive in mindset. We'll call this your *success circle*, and it should include no more than three to five people. These are the ones who are supportive of your plans.

Take note—be careful about choosing those who have been naysayers in the past, because they may provide negative energy you don't need! If you feel that you don't know anyone, this is where a life coach, mentor program, or career counselor can help you in staying accountable to your goals. You can easily search for these types of resources on the Internet using the words mentioned along with the name of your city.

Step Seven: Create a Vision Board

It's a proven fact that viewing images that remind us of what we want helps to bring them into reality. Create a vision board for yourself and notice the power it has over your drive to accomplish your vision.

Collect three to five magazines that contain great pictures. It could be a sports magazine, fashion magazine, family magazine, etc. Cut out pictures that represent your vision. For example, a woman helping children might be the part of your vision of feeding homeless parents and their children, or starting a daycare. Also make sure to include a picture of yourself to place in the middle of your board, so you can get a vision of yourself in the midst of this development. Using a glue stick and a sheet of construction paper or a poster board, paste your pictures in a collage-like fashion on your paper background. Make sure you leave space at the top and around the borders for words and slogans.

Step Eight: Create Your Commitment Affirmation

To keep yourself motivated, inspired, and committed, write a one- to two-sentence affirmation that you can duplicate on three to five index cards. Put them anywhere you need to have access to them: bathroom, car, kitchen, wallet, purse, desk, your favorite chair, etc. Read and repeat out loud your affirmations at least three times daily and three times at each interval. This helps to create a pattern of auto-suggestion that will influence your own attitude and behavior toward that which you desire.

CHAPTER 6

The Power of Goal Setting

"A goal is a dream with a deadline."
Napoleon Hill

Goal setting is an applied process where you plan how you will implement and support your vision. It is an important life technique that millions of people are familiar with but rarely use. It is one of the reasons why so many people leave this world without ever having pursued their dreams at all. In chapter two, "Understanding the Power of Vision," I shared how the world has been shaped and formed by people of vision; but the important thing to remember is that these people didn't just keep their dreams stored in their minds. They transferred them onto paper and set goals in order to make things happen. They took action.

The Benefits of Goal Setting

One of the biggest benefits I have experienced from goal setting in my life is that it gives me clarity. When I write down a new vision and then ask myself the question, "What actions need to happen in order for me to experience my vision?" I feel empowered and I can see my vision coming to life. Another benefit is that you can see your dreams come to reality through goal setting. The actual process of it all transforms your thoughts into action and activates your power and ability to create.

Shaping Your Goals

While many people use the words "vision" and "goal" interchangeably, I believe that goal setting is actually a process that supports your vision. Think about it—first you form a thought, then it takes shape and becomes a goal that you want to experience within a specific time frame. In order for that vision to actually happen, you must then execute a plan of action that will take it from your mind, onto paper, and then into action. Therefore, your goals are shaped by your vision and what you want to experience in life.

When you're making a decision about the goals that will support your vision, make sure you are specific about them.

For example, instead of saying that you want to own a successful business, decide on the type of business that you want to own. If your goal is weight loss, decide on the number of pounds and the time frame you want to lose them in. Remember, a goal is time sensitive. As you shape your goals, it is important to remember that you don't have to do it all by yourself. You might discover that you'll need the help, support, and expertise of other people. Again, if your goal is to lose weight, then you might need the help of a weight loss coach to help hold you accountable. If you want to start a business, then you might need to seek out the help of a business consultant. If you feel a little nervous about setting your goals altogether, then you might need the help of a life coach or someone who has your best interest at heart. You can also seek the guidance of a trusted friend who may have stronger skills in goal setting. Look around you. Who seems to get things done? Who seems to be successful at making things happen? These are the type of people from whom you can seek help.

Be A SMART Goal Setter

You can accomplish anything if you know how to use the power of goal setting. Again, it takes a lot of skill and planning, and that's where the challenge comes in. This is especially the case when you have demons working against you. There needs to be structure and organization. Another technique used by many successful goal setters is called the S-M-A-R-T method. The acronym stands for:

- Specific
- Measureable
- Action
- Realistic
- Time-driven

Specific

Specific means being clear and to the point on what exactly your goal is or will be. While I've given you some examples of being specific earlier in this chapter, consider the goal of an exercise routine. If you wanted to exercise regularly, you would be more specific by saying what type of exercise and perhaps how often. Example: "I will walk for thirty minutes a day, three times per week." Writing in first person will help you to take ownership and stick with the specifics of the length of time and number of days. Now you can schedule this goal in your planner or calendar.

Measurable

It's important to know when you've accomplished your goal, so your results have to be measurable. Example: Once you schedule your daily walks for thirty minutes, three times per week in your calendar, you can then assess whether or not you've completed the goal each day.

Actionable

At the end of the day, it's going to be about whether you were willing to stay committed and take action! Action is a verb, and it means that you must be moving and taking steps toward accomplishing your goals. Achieving your goals has more to do with you taking action than with anything else. You must accept full responsibility for your goals, and blame no one else if they're not achieved. This holds you completely accountable for your success!

Realistic

If you can't see your vision being achieved, then you're not being realistic with the vision or setting goals for it. In order to accomplish any vision, you must believe in it and be able to truly see it come to pass. Be careful not to adopt someone else's vision or falsely create a vision because you think it sounds good or will impress others. Your vision must come from within, and it must be your own thought or idea.

Time-driven

Time management is the partner to goal setting, and it can't be overlooked. You can effectively write down all the goals that will support your dreams, but if you don't set deadlines and plan out your goals in your calendar, this can impair your focus. It will be important to set a deadline for each of your goals—a date for when you would like to complete each one. It's okay if you underestimate. Simply adjust the time frame for accomplishing each of your goals if you truly need to. Now be careful not to use this as a way to procrastinate. Hold yourself accountable and stay committed to getting things done.

Eliminating Goal-Setting Failure

Napoleon Hill once said, "A goal is a dream with a deadline." What separates the doers from dreamers is that doers take action with their goals. You can be good at dreaming or visioning all day long. However, if you can't get your vision to the planning phase and take the necessary steps to achieve the goal, then you won't achieve it! Knowing and understanding this fact is vital to your goal-setting success.

I believe there are five common reasons why most people fail to reach their goals. They are:

1. Your goals don't support your vision

It's important to make sure that the goals you set are really yours and that they support your vision. In other words, keep it real with yourself! It's not uncommon to adopt the things that others want for us. This influence may come from your spouse, family members, or friends. When the goal really isn't yours from the start, it's a lot easier to let it "fall through the cracks" and not accomplish it. Make sure your goals are in alignment with your vision and that the vision is truly what you believe in and not what others want for you!

2. Lack of planning

Maybe you've heard the expression failing to plan is planning to fail. It's a true statement, and the lack of planning can hold your vision and goals back more than anything else. Planning is the beginning stage of taking action. It gets the vision out of your thought process and onto paper, and, from there, you can set your goals.

3. Forgetting why you set the goal

It's not uncommon for some goals to take months or even years to complete. Many of your goals will depend on your skill level and whether or not you need to create subgoals to gain those skills. This can cause you to procrastinate and put off the goal, and, with time, you may forget why you set the goal in the first place. This is why you must be able to see your vision clearly and know that it is based on what you truly want.

4. Too Busy Being Busy!

Let's face it—life can be in the fast lane sometimes, and, depending on what your obligations are to your family, prior commitments, and other activities, you could be just too busy being busy! You'll have to decide on what you really want at this point and time in your life and what you're willing to give up to have it. You'll also need to better structure your time and stick with mapping out your goals and your to-do items on your calendar.

5. Fear

One of the affirmations that I recommend, in chapter four, that you learn and repeat throughout your day in dealing with fear is, "I am only limited to the size of my dreams and the scope of my vision. My dreams are bigger than my doubts and greater than my fears." Fear in goal setting basically has to do with you not believing that you can accomplish the goal you've set, or the goal is so big that you are overwhelmed and not quite sure how to make it happen. This is where proper planning comes into play. If you divide your goals and break them down into smaller subgoals and daily to-do items, you'll get closer to accomplishing them. Once you map out your goals in your calendar, you'll have more clarity and gain control of your fear.

As you read this book and get a better understanding of the importance and difference visioning can make in your life, you must understand that visioning and goal setting go together. Your vision could just remain dormant in your mind, and, if never implemented, you very well may leave this world with all of your talent and potential never put into action.

Therefore, you must be the one to implement your vision by taking action! Executing the power of goal setting will help you to do just that. This powerful technique can help you to accomplish your vision faster and more efficiently. It will also teach you the importance of structure and discipline in planning. Now, just as it will take you time to eliminate the D.E.M.O.N.S. contributing to habits that prevent you from exploring your true potential, it will take you time to fine-tune your goal-setting skills as well. Be patient with yourself. Seek the help of others who might know more about this process and who are willing to share. Remember, you are in control of your goals and you can adjust them as you see the need. I have included worksheets in this chapter to help facilitate your goal-setting process. Please use them, because they will help you to strengthen your skills in utilizing this powerful and necessary technique.

Putting It All Together

My sincere hope and prayer is that, after reading *Vision Power*, you have found it to be helpful in a significant way. In the spirit of goal setting, it has been my attempt to empty myself and to share with you a very methodical and strategic way to enrich yourself and to make your thoughts realities. The time invested into writing my own experience is a personal way of expressing thanks to the God of heaven who enabled me and safeguarded my way through many dark places, toils, and snares. What I discovered along the way with many reckless adventures, setbacks, and failures is that there are better ways, tried and true, to reach your objectives, particularly the ones of achievement and success on a higher plane. While there are some who stumble upon success and perhaps find it through serendipity, there are others who discover it through hard work, proper planning, and effective time management, which are all necessary to achieve your desired goals. In this twenty-first century, the society we live in and its present generation seek instant gratification. Many yearn for their dreams and visions to appear and manifest instantaneously. Life is not a fairytale, but, with the proper planning, you can indeed bring your vision to light, reach your goals, and live your dream!

Don't Procrastinate, Get Started!

Within the pages of this book are the strategies for building a more abundant and successful life. The first thing is to start where you are right now. Make up your mind that you want more for yourself and for your loved ones. Make sure that you have read this book in sequential order, completing the recommended exercises and worksheets. Remember, you can't erect the framework of a house until the foundation is laid. The foundation for creating your vision is in establishing first things first. The objective is for you to fully grasp the concepts discussed in the preceding chapters and follow the timeless principles shared, which can lead you to the golden ring that so many long to touch.

Getting to a Better Place!

Your story or your motivation for change could be entirely different from my story, as I shared with you in chapter one. It does not matter what your circumstances might be, the point is that you can get to a better place from here, and it's all up to you! The future is yours to put your own stamp on and make your vision and your dreams a reality. It can be done, and I can assure you it's your time to do it. If it weren't, then you wouldn't be reading this book. I want to see you accomplish spectacular things. Today is the day you begin redesigning your own life and living day-to-day with the desire to have a more fulfilling existence. The time has come. No more excuses, no more doubt, and no more aimless living for you.

It's your time to shine!

APPENDIX

Your 21-Day Action Plan

Now that you have a better understanding of what a vision is and the importance of finding your purpose, it's time to put it all into a system that you will be able to hold yourself accountable to. The 21-Day Action Plan is not about you feeling rushed to develop your vision within the twenty-one-day time frame, it is meant simply as a guide that allows you to do a little each day, which in turn will help you to accomplish writing your vision and began living your dreams. If you feel that you need more time, simply slow it down and work on one action at a time until you have completed them all.

Day 1: Self-Discovery

Set some time aside to answer the following questions and write your thoughts down. Remember, be perfectly honest with yourself! After going through the various exercises and asking yourself the hard questions, what do you know now that you did not know concerning the obstacles in your way? Have you gotten glimpses of a new and better self? Self-discovery is the bedrock for all the other steps in this twenty-one-day plan.

Am I satisfied with my life and what I'm doing at this time?

Write the truth about your present state and identify exactly what it is that you are dissatisfied about and what you plan on doing about it.

_____

_____

_____

_____

_____

_____

_____

If my answer is no, what would I like to be doing?

Write your dreams and your vision, whether you have the plan at this time or not.

_____

_____

_____

_____

_____

_____

_____

_____

If my answer is yes, what do I want to do more of or do next?

_____

_____

_____

_____

_____

_____

What am I passionate about? (i.e., What do you love doing even if you don't get paid for it?)

_____

_____

_____

_____

_____

_____

_____

_____

What do people compliment me on most often?

_____

_____

_____

_____

_____

_____

_____

What are my talents?

_____

_____

_____

_____

_____

_____

_____

What are my interests?

_____

_____

_____

_____

_____

_____

_____

What are my hobbies?

_____

_____

_____

_____

_____

_____

_____

Day 2: Eliminating Your D.E.M.O.N.S.

Now it's time to identify the demons that are holding you back from finding your true purpose and developing your vision. Remember, demons can be roadblocks, clutter, and obstructions in your way that surround you. For each of the eight demons that I mention, please share your feelings about how each of them is impacting your life. Next, you'll write a solution for how you will work on getting rid of them. These are the demons that are blocking your blessings.

1. The Demon of Doubt

_____

_____

_____

_____

_____

_____

_____

_____

2. The Demon of Fear

_____

_____

_____

_____

_____

_____

_____

_____

Day 3: Eliminating Your D.E.M.O.N.S. (2nd Day)

3. The Demon of Bad Habits

_____

_____

_____

_____

_____

_____

_____

4. The Demon of Excuses

_____

_____

_____

_____

_____

_____

_____

_____

Day 4: Eliminating Your D.E.M.O.N.S. (3rd Day)

5. The Demon of Procrastination

_____

_____

_____

_____

_____

_____

_____

_____

6. The Demon of Distraction

_____

_____

_____

_____

_____

_____

_____

_____

_____

Day 5: Eliminating Your D.E.M.O.N.S. (4th Day)

7. The Demon of Guilt

_____

_____

_____

_____

_____

_____

_____

_____

8. The Demon of Negative Relationships

_____

_____

_____

_____

_____

_____

_____

_____

Day 6: The Search for Light in A Dark, Quiet Room

If you'll remember from chapter four, spending a day by yourself free from distraction in a comfortable, dark, quiet room is very important. It allows you to center yourself and search the inner sanctum of your soul, searching for your blessing blockers and your mentally embedded distractions that are obscuring your new self.

Write Down Your Experience

What did you discover about yourself in that dark, quiet place? It's time now to begin putting together your personally designed life based upon your talents, strengths, and abilities. You have identified your weaknesses and hang-ups and have resolved to eradicate them by any means necessary.

_____

_____

_____

_____

_____

_____

_____

Day 7: The Search for Light in a Dark, Quiet Room (2nd Day)

Write Down Your Experience

_____

_____

_____

_____

_____

_____

_____

_____

_____

Day 8: The Search for Light in a Dark, Quiet Room (3rd Day)

Write Down Your Experience

_____

_____

_____

_____

_____

_____

_____

_____

_____

Day 9 Through Day 13: Writing Your Vision

Writing your vision will help you to gain clarity and focus on what you really want to do. It's all about what you want to experience at some point and time in your life. Remember, you can have a short-term vision (one month to one year) or a long-term vision (years). It's all up to you and in your total control. It's also not uncommon to have a vision for different areas in your life. The most important thing to remember is that a vision is about what you would like to experience. There are also no length requirements for writing your vision. You do not have to write pages or even paragraphs; it's all up to you. And the beautiful thing is that you can always revise it.

Six areas to consider when thinking about your vision:

1. Education/Learning
2. Family/Friends
3. Health
4. Financial
5. Spiritual
6. Career

In the space provided, please write your vision:

_____

_____

_____

_____

_____

_____

_____

_____

_____

_____

Day 14: Creating Goals to Support Your Vision

Be reminded that there are short-term, intermediate, and long-range goals.

The tasks we perform in the short-term lead us to the long-term objective. It is obvious that reaching our destiny is accomplished by one step at a time. Taking care of the little things on the path leading to the big thing is absolutely necessary.

If your goal is to reach a certain point in a particular time frame, there are tasks you need to do daily, weekly, and monthly as you move toward your goal. Completing these tasks in a timely fashion and accomplishing these objectives in between is how this works.

This method is a simple, methodical way of realizing your dream and your vision and reaching your goal within the time you have allotted. Having a consistent, systematic way of getting things done that are important to you is a smart, time-saving, and powerful strategy. By keeping your eye on the prize and doing one task at a time, you get closer and closer to the thing you want. The question is always the same. What do you want? And when do you want it?

Vision-Supporting Goals

_____

_____

_____

_____

_____

_____

_____

_____

_____

_____

Day 15: Creating Goals to Support Your Vision (2nd day)

Vision-Supporting Goals

_____

_____

_____

_____

_____

_____

_____

_____

_____

Day 16: Write Any Challenges You Face in Accomplishing Your Goals

Identifying and finding solutions to challenges will help you to accomplish your goals faster. Not setting short-term, intermediate, and long-term goals can be a hindrance in reaching your objectives.

_____

_____

_____

_____

_____

_____

_____

_____

Day 17: Write the Solutions for Any Challenges

List the thing or things that need to be eradicated in order to move forward.

Goal-Challenge Solutions

_____

_____

_____

_____

_____

_____

_____

Day 18: Staying the Course

Identify skills that you might need to improve upon or people that you'll need to get help from to accomplish your goals. Note: If you don't know the name of the person, simply write down the service or help needed.

Goal Skill(s) or Resources Needed

_____

_____

_____

_____

_____

_____

_____

_____

Days 19 and 20: Create Your Vision Board

Supplies Needed:

- 8.5 x 11 sheet of paper

- Old magazines with lots of pictures

- Glue stick

Flip through the magazines and cut out pictures that reflect your vision. Next, using the sheet of paper and glue stick, place the pictures on the paper either in order of importance or in a collage. Once you have completed your vision board, make color copies of it and place it in areas where you'll be constantly reminded of your commitment.

Day 21: Staying Committed

Congratulations, you are on your way to accomplishing your vision! Write down ways you can stay faithful and committed to your vision:

1. Read your affirmations of commitment repeatedly

2. Hold your new mental image of the changed person you are becoming.

3. It is your life—why not make it the best life?

4. Pray without ceasing that the wisdom and guidance of God reign supreme in your life.

_____

_____

_____

_____

_____

_____

_____

_____

_____

About the Author

Edward L. Keyton is the minister emeritus to the Church of Christ on Bouldercrest Road in Atlanta, Georgia. Having served there successfully over twenty-six years, Keyton is an accomplished preacher, motivator, and entrepreneur.